Divine Dialogue

JOHNSON F. ODESOLA

authorHOUSE®

AuthorHouse™
1663 Liberty Drive
Bloomington, IN 47403
www.authorhouse.com
Phone: 1 (800) 839-8640

Published by AuthorHouse 12/27/2019

ISBN: 978-1-7283-4139-2 (sc)
ISBN: 978-1-7283-4138-5 (e)

Print information available on the last page.

This book is printed on acid-free paper.

Scripture taken from The Holy Bible, King James Version. Public Domain

DEDICATION

This book is dedicated to Daddy and Mummy E. A. Adeboye under whom I learnt the art of praying. They wrote at the blank table of my life by their exemplary lives of devotion.

ACKNOWLEDGEMENT

I am am indebted to several people who have to the reality of this book. My contributed beloved wife Adebisi for her advise; Pastor E. A. Odeyemi, my immediate boss for his unswerving encouragement. My special thanks goes to members of staff of C.R.M. who proof read, and supervised the printing to bring it to the final stage as it is now.

TABLE OF CONTENTS

PREFACE

W e are in the era that telephone to glory is like a spare Tyre: we resort to it after human knowledge and endeavors have failed. How often the Lord's work suffers and languishes because we do not dial the direct line to God. What a terrible thing that God's people live in poverty, in sickness, in disappointment and defeat because they do not telephone the Headquarters of God.

Our heavenly Father says that the gold and silver are His and the cattle on thousands hills. He has lovingly invited us to tell Him all our needs. He says:"What things so ever you desire, when you pray". He promised us "great and mighty things which thou knowest not" (Jer. 33:3). Yet we live at a poor dying rate in physical, mental and spiritual bankruptcy. We do not have because we do not ask. Our mouths are never full because we never need. Will you today take to heart His blessed promises and begin your telephone to glory now? It will be amazing to you the response that will come from the heavenly Headquarters.

It is my prayer that your blessing and benefits need. Will you today take to heart His blessed promises and begin your telephone to glory now? It will be amazing to you the response that will come from the heavenly Headquarters.

It is my prayer that your blessing and benefits

Chapter 1

THE VENTURE
OF
PRAYER

THE VENTURE OF PRAYER

Prayer is a common but unnatural activity. From birth we have been learning the rules of self-reliance as we strain and struggle to achieve self-sufficiency. Prayer, in the face of those deep-seated values, is an assault on human autonomy, and an indictment of independent living. To people in the fast lane, who determine to make it on their own, prayer is an embarrassing interruption.

Prayer is alien to our proud human nature. Yet somewhere, sometime, probably all of us reach the pints of falling to our knees bowing our heads, focusing our attention of God, praying. We may look both ways to be sure no-one is watching; we may blush; but in spite of foreignness of the activity, we pray.

Why Are We Drawn To Prayer?

There could be two possible explanations to this: The Inexplicable Firstly, by intuition or experience we understand that the most intimate communion with God comes only through prayer. Ask people who have faced tragedy or trial, heart-break or grief, failure or defeat, loneliness or discrimination. Ask what happened in their souls when they finally fell on their knees and poured out their hearts to the Lord. Such people have often said, "I can't explain it, but I felt as though God understood me".

Others have said, "I felt surrounded by His presence". Or "I felt a comfort and peace I have never felt before." The apostle Paul knew this experience. Writing to the Christians at Philip he said. "Do not be anxious about anything, but in everything, by prayer and supplication, with thanksgiving, present your requests to God. And the peace of God, which passeth all understanding, will guard your hearts and your minds in Christ Jesus." (Phil. 4:6-7).

By Prayer

Prayer has not always been my strong point – for many years. Even as an assistant pastor in a well-established church. I knew more about prayer than practiced in my own life. I have a racehorse temperament, and the tug of self-sufficiency and self-reliance are a way real to me. I didn't want to get off the fast track long enough to find out what prayer is all about.

Several years ago, the Holy Spirit gave me a leading so direct that I couldn't ignore, argue against, or disobey it. The leading was to explore, study and practice prayer until I finally understand it. This I did by moving closely with my father in the Lord, his wife and my immediate boss. And then I did something radical: I prayed. The greatest fulfillment in my prayer life has not been the list of miraculous answer to prayers I have received, although that has been wonderful. The greatest thrill has been the qualitative difference in my relationship with God. And when I started to pray, I didn't know that was going to happen.

God and I used to be rather usually related to one another. We didn't get together and talk very much. Now, however, we get together a lot, not talking on the run, but by substantial, soul- searching conversations every morning for a good deal of time. Without doubt I have known God a lot better since I have started praying.

If the Holy Spirit is leading you to learn more about prayer, you are about to embark on a wonderful venture. As you grow in prayer, God will reveal more of Himself to you, breathe more of His life into your spirit. That will be the most fulfilling and rewarding part of your experience with prayer. More so even than the answers to prayer you are sure to receive. Fellowship with God, trust, confidence, peace, relief are the wonderful requests the will become yours as you learn to pray.

A Pipeline for God's Power

Though prayer, God gives us His peace. This alone should make this self-sufficient twentieth century people to fall on their knees pouring out their hearts to Him. But there is another reason. People are drawn to prayer because they know that God's power flow primarily to people who pray.

The scripture are riddled with passages teaching that our Almighty, omnipotent God is able, willing and ready to answer the prayers of His followers. The miracles of Israelite's Exodus from Egypt and subsequent journey to the promise land were all enough evidences to the fact that He answers prayer. So were Jesus' miracles of raising the dead. As the early church formed, grew continual prayers for healing and deliverance, God's power can change circumstances and relationships. It can help us to face life's daily struggles. It can heal psychological and physical problems, remove marriage obstruction, and meet financial needs. In fact, it can handle any kind of difficulty, dilemma and discouragement.

Prayer as War Strategy

I want to draw your attention to an Old Testament story that has persuaded me more than any other Biblical passage that prayer has significant result. It is found in Exodus 17:8-13:

"Then call Amalek, and fought with Israel in Rephidin. And Moses said unto Joshua choose us out men and, go out, fight with Amalek, tomorrow. I will stand on the top of the hill with the rod of God in mine hand. So Joshua did as Moses had said to him and fought with Amalek; and Moses, Aaron, and Hur went up to the tope of the Hill and it came to pass, when Moses held up his hands, that Israel prevailed. But Moses hands were heavy; and they took stone, and put it under him, and he sat thereon; and Aaron and Hur stayed up his hands, the one on the side, and the other on the other side; and his hands were steady until the going down of the sun. And Joshua discomfited Amalek and his people with the edge of the sword."

Moses, Israel famous leader was faced with a crisis. An enemy army has just arrived near Israelis desert camp, intent on wiping out Israel. Moses called in his most capable military leader for a discussion of military strategy. After a thorough planning session, Moses announces the approach they will take. Joshua, he says "tomorrow, you take the best fighting men we have and lead them out on the plains to meet the enemy: and fight with courage. I am going to take two men with me, climb the hill that over-look the plains, and raise my hands towards heaven. I am going to pray that God will pour out courage, valor, coordination and supernatural protection on our troops. Then I am going to watch and see what God does".

Energy through Prayer

Joshua agrees. He believes in prayer and he would rather have Moses prayer support than his military support. What happens, of course is that when Moses' hands are stretched heavenwards, Joshua's troops prevail in battle, fighting with a divine intensity that drives back the enemy. But as can be expected, Moses' arm grew weary. He dropped them to his sides and walked around the Hill, viewing the battle shifted right before his eyes. Joshua's troops are being struck down, the enemy was gaining ground.

Moses stretched his arms towards heaven again and brought the matter to the Lord. Immediately the battle's momentum shifts back to Joshua and the Israelite, and once again they were driving the enemy back. And then it struck Moses, He must keep his arms stretched towards heaven in prayer if he wanted to open the door for God's supernatural intervention on the battle field. Moses discovered that day that God's prevailing power is revealed through prayer. When I began praying in earnest, I discovered the same thing it boils down to this; if you are willing to invite God to involve Himself in your daily challenges, you will experience His prevailing power. In your home, in your relationships, in the market place, in the school, in the church, and wherever it is most needed. That power may come in the form of wisdom, an idea you desperately need and cannot come up with yourself. It may come in the form of courage greater than you could ever muster. It may come in the form of confidence or perseverance, uncommon staying power, a change attitude towards a wife or a child or a parent, change in circumstance, may be even outright miracles. Whenever it comes, God's prevailing power is released in the lives of people who pray.

You Are Not For Defeat

Not to surrender is the other side of the equation and it is sobering; it is hard for God to release His power upon your life when you drop your arms to your side, put your hand in your pocket and say. "I can handle it on my own." If you do that, do not be surprised if one day you get the nagging feeling that the tide of the battle has shifted against you, that you are powerless to do anything about it.

Prayer-less people cut themselves off from God's prevailing power, and the frequent result in the familiar feeling of being overwhelmed, over-run, beaten down, pushed around and defeated. Surprising numbers of people are willing to settle for lives like that. But why should you be one of them? Nobody desire to live like that. Prayer is the key to unlocking God's prevailing power in your life.

Once Moses made the connection between prayer and God's power, he determined to spend the rest of the day praying for God's involvement in the battle. But his arms grew weary. He knew better that to drop them in his sides; he had done that and watches his troops got wiped out. So the two men who accompanied him up the hill found a stone he could sit on. Then each man crawled under an arm and helped Moses being supported by caring people who wanted to help him keeps the power flowing! Needless to say, Israel won the battle that day.

Are you weary of praying? Do you feel that your prayers are ineffective? Do you wonder if God is really listening? In this book I will like to play the role of one of Moses' friends, Telephone operator, helping you hold up your arms until the day is done and the victory is yours. I will like to be used by God to inspire you to pray, no matter how discouraged you may feel right now.

I know that God hears and answers prayer. He answers mine and he will answer yours too; if you can telephone to Him in Glory. Your venture of prayer begins with His willingness to listen.

The Prayer Structure

According to a well-known business axion, if you want to know something, ask an expert. I make sense, then, if you want to be schooled how to pray, ask the number one expert – Jesus Christ Himself.

No one in history has even understood prayer better than Jesus – No one has ever believed more strongly in the power of prayer, and no one has ever prayed as He did. His disciples recognized His expertise. Once they stumble upon Him while He was praying (Luke 11:1). They were so moved by His earnestness and intensity that when He finally got up from His knees, one of them timidly asked, would you teach and give us a pattern for prayer? They knew that in comparison to their Master they were infants in the school of prayer.

A Pattern For Prayer

In other to have a solid structure, you need a plan to avoid derailment. This is also true of prayer; you need a pattern to avoid becoming unbalanced. Without a routine, you will probably fall into the "Please God" trap: please God, give me please God, help me, Please God, love me. Please God, arrange this and that occasionally you render a few thanks heaven wards when you notice that God has allowed some good things to come your way. Once a while, when your sin finds you out you confess and forsake and if you are feeling really spiritual, you might even throw a little worship into your prayers, but only as the spirit leads.

If I sound sarcastic, it is because I know about unbalanced prayer: I am not an expert in it, if I am anything in this school; I am still in the elementary stage. But I can tell you from personal experience where unbalanced prayer leads. Sensing the carelessness and one sidedness of your prayers, you begin to feel guilty about praying. Guilt leads to faint-heartedness, and that in turn leads to prayerlessness. When prayer praying makes you feel guilty, you may soon stop praying.

If something near this has happened to you. It is time to set up a prayer routine. I am going to offer you a pattern to follow. It is not the only pattern or perfect pattern, but it is a good pattern that has been used for many years in Christians circles. It is balance and it is easy. What you need to remember is ACTS, this acrostic stands for:
*Adoration
*Confession
*Thanksgiving and
*Supplication

Open the Door of Prayer with Adoration

It is absolutely essential to begin time of prayer with adoration or worship. There are many reasons for this but I will mention four here:-

1. Adoration sets the tone for the entire prayer
    It reminds us whom we are addressing, whose presence we have entered, whose attention we have gained. How often our problems, trial, temptation and needs seem so pressing that we reduce prayer to a wish list! But when we commit ourselves to beginning all our prayers with adoration, we have to low down and focus our attention on God.

Walking into some churches, we are gripped for a moment. We say to ourselves, "This is holy ground. I need to concentrate, to focus on what is going on here." Our initial pause add to the service that follows. Likewise, when we begin our prayer with adoration, we set the tone for our meeting with God.

2. Adoration reminds us of God's identity and inclination
As we list His attributes, lifting up His character and personality, we reinforced our understandings of who He is.

At various times, I begin my prayer by saying, "I worship your Majesty and You for Omnipotence." When I say that, I am reminded that God is able to solve problems, and help me, no matter how difficult my situation may be. I also worship Him for His Omnipresence. Wherever I am praying, in the car, in the air or on the sea and in the village, I know He is there with me. I worship Him for His Omniscience. No mystery confounds God; He will not have to scratch His Head about anything I say.

3. Adoration purifies the one who is praying
When you have spent a few minutes praising God for who He is, your spirit softens and your agenda changes. Those burning issues you were dying to bring to God's attention may seem less crucial. Your sense of desperation subsides as you focus on God's greatness, and you can truly say, "I am enjoying you. God, it is well with my soul" Adoration purges your spirit and prepares you to listen to God.

4. God is worthy of adoration

It should be hard to get past the "Our Father" in your prayer without falling back in awe at that miracle. "How great is the love the Father has lavished on us, that we should be called Children of God!" (I John 3:1) A God who is Omnipotent, who is Omniscient and Omnipresence and yet Who loves us, watches over us, gives us good gifts – this is amazing! Our heavenly Father is worthy of all our worship, and so right at the beginning let us offer it to Him.

Way To Adore God

How do you adore God? What better way than to list its attributes? Sometimes I think of every attributes I can. Some other times I focus on one, I have been especially aware of in recent times when facing major decisions, I can concentrate on His guidance. When suffering from a feeling of inadequacy or guilt, I may praise Him for His mercy. When in need, I may worship Him for His providence and power.

Pick out a Psalm of praise and ready or say it to Him. Some of the best known are Psalms 8, 19, 23, 46, 95, 100 and 148 – but go through the whole book and see what you can find. Other wonderful Psalms of praise are in Luke 1: 40-45 and Zecchariah's song (Lk 1:68-79). And if you are in a close room, sing to God songs of praises.

Adoration is foreign to most twentieth-century believers. You may feel dry when you start. Like anything else you embark upon fresh-new job or computer programming – you have to get disciplined, stretch and work at it to do it well. "What is worth doing at all is what doing well." After sometime you will gain both comfort and proficiency. Adoration becomes a necessity in your prayer life. You can no longer get along without it.

Confession: A Neglected Art

Confession is probably the most neglected area in personal prayer today. We often hear people pray publicly, "Lord, forgive us our many sins." A host of us carry that approach to our private prayer. We throw all our sins on to a pile, without so much as looking at them and we say, "God please cover the whole dirty heap."

This approach to confession, unfortunately is a colossal cop-out when I lump up all my sins together and confess them en-masse, it is not too painful or embarrassing. But if I take those sins out of the pile one by one and call them by name, I make whole lot of difference.

I determine that in my prayers, I would deal with sin specifically. I would say, "I told so and so there were about one thousand people in the meeting. When in the actual figure they were Nine hundred and ninety. That was a lie, and therefore I am a liar. I plead for your forgiveness for being a liar. OR instead of admitting I had been less than the best husband, I would say, "Today I willfully determined to be self-centered, uncaring and insensitive. It was a deliberate or intentional act. I walk through the door thinking. I desire to have things in my own way." I need your forgiveness for the sin of selfishness.

When we are honest with God, your conscience will be cleansed; you will be flooded with relief that God has forgiving nature. Knowing that "as far as the east is from the west, so far has He removed our transgression from us" (Psalm 103:12), then you can learn the deep meaning of peace. With this peace you are liberated to pray by the power of the Holy Ghost to ask for anything.

Expressing Thanks

The T in ACTS stands for thanksgiving, Psalm 103:2 says: "Praise the Lord, O my soul, and forget not all His benefits." Apostle Paul also writes in I Thessalonians 5:18, "Give thanks in all circumstance for this is God's will for you in Christ Jesus."

Some of us have not made a simple distinction. There is difference between feeling grateful and expressing thanks. The classic teaching on this is in Luke 17:11-19; the story of the ten men healed of leprosy. How many of those men do you think felt tremendous gratitude as they walked away from Jesus completely healed of their incurable, disgusting, socially isolating disease? There is no question about it, all ten did. But how many came back, threw themselves at Jesus' feet and thanked Him? Just one!

In this story we catch a glimpse of Jesus' emotions. He was moved first to be disappointed by people who felt grateful but did not take the time to express it. Second to satisfaction by the one who came all the way back to say, thank you. Parents, you know how it feels when one of your children spontaneously thank you for something. God is our Father, and He too is moved when we express our thanksgiving.

I thank God every day for four kinds of blessings – answered prayers, spiritual blessings, relational blessings and material blessings. Almost everything in my life fits into one of those categories.

Asking For Assistance

But then it is time for supplication-requests. Philippians 4:6 says, "Be careful for nothing: but in everything by prayer and supplication with thanksgiving let your request be made known unto God." If you have adored Him, confessed your sins and thanked Him for all His good and marvelous works and gifts, you must be ready to tell Him your needs.

Nothing is too big for God to handle or too small for Him to be interested in. Still, I sometimes wonder if my requests are legitimate. So I am honest with God. I say, "Lord I do not know if I have the rights to ask for this or I do not know how to pray about that. But I lift it up to you. Let your Holy Spirit help me to pray in your own way."

God honors that kind of prayer. James says; "If any of you lack wisdom, he should ask God, who gives generously to all without finding fault; and it will be given to him." (James 1:5).

At other times, when I think I know how to pray, I say "God, this is my heart on the matter: You have asked me to make my request known. This actually is what I am doing. My requests are broken down into categories; Ministry people, family and personal.

Under MINISTRY, I pray for my father in the Lord, our church as a whole, the states of my operation as the Senior Pastor, Holy Ghost Services, camp expansion and the sub-ministries of our church. I pray that through our church and the ministry God will draw people to Himself. Also that the end time Revival that will usher in the Lord, that God has started through us will not stop.

Under PEOPLE, I pray for brethren in Leadership positions, Missionaries, Departments, Boards, the sick; I pray for the unsaved people in my circle of youthful friends, that God will draw them to himself.

Under FAMILY, I pray for my marriage and for my children, I ask God to make me a godly husband. I ask Him for help about decisions, finances and so on.

Under PERSONAL, I pray about my character. I say, God, I want to be more Holy and righteous. I want to be a vessel of honor, a dependable and loyal minister in the work of the Lord. Whatever you have to bring into life to clip away my character, bring it on. I want to be conformed to the image of Christ.

Break up your requests into whatever categories that suit your purposes, and then keep a list of what you have prayed about. After a month go back and re-read your list.

Find out what God has already done, in many cases, you will be amazed.

Acts Methods In Prayer

I have found the ACTS formula helpful especially when I write out my prayer points. Starting with adoration, saying; "good morning, Lord, I feel fine to praise you today. I am choosing this moment when I am fresh and ready, willing and preparing for the day assignment, to stop and say that I love you. You are a wonderful God. Your personality and character bring me to my knees. You are Holy, just, righteous gracious, merciful, fatherly and forgiving. I am happy and joyful to be in relationship with you today, and I worship you Now."

After adoration, I move to confession, "Please forgive me for committing the sin of partiality. It is so much easier for me to direct my love and attention toward those seem to "have it all together" without even realizing it, I find myself avoiding trouble people. I am sorry. Thanks for your impartiality to me. Please forgive me, and now I claim your forgiveness, thank you for forgiving me."

The T thanksgiving is easy for me. I thank God for specific answers to prayer, for helping me in my work, for people's responsiveness, for material and relational blessings and for anything also that makes me particularly happy. Thanking the Lord every day keeps me from being covetous; retrospection into his goodness reminds me of the vast number of blessing I enjoy.

I am glad that S supplication is last. Once I have worshipped God, confessed my sins, and given thanks, it is now time to take out my shopping list.

In fact James 4:2 says, "You do not have, because you do not ask God." I used to be vague about what I needed. But that has changed now. I list specific requests, leave them with God and regularly review them to see how He has answered them.

When I get up from the place of prayer, I feel as if a load has been lifted off from my shoulders. I Peter 5:7 says; "Casting all your care upon Him, for He careth for you." When I pray, I am not just telling God my problems, I am turning my biggest concern over to Him. Once I have put them in His capable hands, I can go about my day in His strength, free from crouching concerns.

Chapter 2

TELEPHONE
TO
GLORY

TELEPHONE TO GLORY

"Be careful for nothing; but in everything by prayer and supplication with thanksgiving let your request be made known unto God"- Phil. 4:6.

God and prayer are inseparable. The unbelieving world expect to get things by work or by planning or by scheming or by accidents; but God's children are taught that they are to get things by asking and that the reason we do not have is because we do not ask. Belief in God and in prayer is elemental and intuitive. The idea look crude and cruel in this so called civilized times, but the instructional manual of God for our correct functioning is full of the subject of prayer. Everywhere there are commands and inducements to pray and great stories of deliverance and victory, experiences and vision are all examples of prevailing prayer. All crises in the life of our Lord were linked with special seasons of prayer and His teaching set forth wonderful assistances to those who pray. He laid down the law of prayer though He never sought to explain its mystery. Prayer was not a problem to Him. The two parables He spoke about prayers are not very acceptable to those who pray. There is something strange to the spirit of prayer in linking God, to a heartless judge of a churlish friend. God is neither. The parables were spoken as a representative of God, but to illustrate the reward of importunity. The basis of prayer is sonship. Prayer is possible and reasonable because it is natural for a child to ask from his father, and it is also reasonable for the father to listen to the request of his child;

> "If ye then, being evil, know how to give good gifts unto your children how much more shall your father which is in Heaven give good things to them that ask Him" (Matt. 7:7-11, 1 Thess. 6:9-13).

There are many problems about prayer and apart from praying there is no solution. Prayer is a fact of experience; telephone to dear Heavenly father, through all the ages, testimonies of those who prayed have been that God hears and answers prayers of His children.

- Prayer is asking and the answer is receiving
- Prayer is seeking and the answer is finding
- Prayer is knocking and the answer if having;

God opens the door to you. Let us dial the number of our Heavenly Father table telephone, oh what a joy unspeakable to be assessable to the measurable goodies of Heaven.

The Prayer Answering God

We must understand that God hear and answer prayer; God is a living God, He is not an idol or wood or stone or paper. When the priest of Baal on Mount Carmel cried out to their god, there was none who neither answered nor regarded. (I Kings 18:28-36). an idol has eye, but it sees not. It has ears but it hears not. It has a mouth but it speaks not. A God who hears prayer is a living God. God is an all knowing God. Omniscient, Does God hear the cry of millions of His people in all nations, in all languages at the same time?

Does He even know the hearts of the suppliants? Does He see the faith? Does He know the sincerity or hypocrisy in the hearts of those who pray? Then He is a limitless God who knows all things. He has all power in Heaven and on Earth. If God answer prayer for rain, He must control weather. If He answers prayer about crops, He must control the sun, the insects, the moisture, and even the germ of life in the seed itself. God answer prayer about heart, because He has hand in every corpuscle in the blood, every nerve, every process of metabolism in the human body, He also answers prayer about revival and conversion of sinners. He has influence on the very soul's consciences and wills of men. If God answer the prayer of Joshua so that the sun stood still in its relation to the earth for about the space of a day (Josh. 10:12-13) then God controls the whole infinite universe He answer prayer; He has infinite power, limitless power.

God has infinite wisdom, and Almighty power, and then He Himself must be the creator. There could be none as powerful, there could be none to dispute His right, and there could be none other to limit His work or cross His will; a God answering prayer, God the creator of Heaven and the Earth.

This same God who answers is a miracle-working God. To believe that God is a rewarder of them that diligently seek Him means that one has faith in all that is ever claimed from God. His work is miraculous, Supernatural not ordinary but extraordinary, not human but divine, not limited but infinite in scope.

"Does God work miracle today?" Someone asks. The answer is Yes. Because He is still the God who hears and answers prayer, then His ordinary and natural way of working in answering prayers could be miracle. Every time God intervenes and controls nature or changes a plan to make it rain when otherwise would not have rained, and does it because someone prayed then it is a miracle. Every time a person gets well in answer to prayer when otherwise He would not have gotten well, it is a miracle, a divine intervention in natural affairs.

The God of infinite love and mercy will answer our phone call anytime. God knows that none of us deserve to have our prayer answered, we poor sinners deserve only condemnation, forsaking and punishment by death! But God loves sinners. His mercies are boundless. "Where sins abounded, grace did much more abound" (Romans 5:20). If there is a God who rewards those who diligently seek Jim, that is, who hears and answers the cry, the faith, the need of human beings, then God would give His own son alone for sin and make it so He could righteously forgive sin and save sinners and keep them out of hell, and make them into His own image and have them forever with Him in Heaven! Oh, when one really believes that God is a prayer- hearing, prayer-answering God, he/she has secret to the very heart of God, and he can see and outline all the grace and power and majesty of the infinite God. This God who bears and answers prayers is a kind God. Any god who does not hear and answer prayer has not the power and grace to create, support the world, or to love and seek and save lost sinners.

Then if God is a God who hears and answers prayers, let us pray! Prayer then becomes the most, compelling duty of the Christian. God never commanded us to sing without ceasing, nor preach without ceasing: nor give without ceasing: but He did commanded, "Pray without ceasing" (I Thess.5:17). the apostles after Pentecost demanded the selection of deacons that the apostle might give themselves to prayer and the ministry of the word (Acts 6:4). Not first the preaching, but first that they should give themselves to prayer.

> "O thou that hearest prayer, unto thee shall all flesh come" (Psalm 65:2)

The Mind Of God About Prayer

The thought of God are not as man's thought neither are His ways are man's ways. "As the heaven are higher than the earth, so are my ways higher than your ways and my thoughts than your thoughts." (Isaiah 55:9). God has made known His thoughts and His ways in the revelation of His words and in the person of His Son. God has never put His thoughts into a thesis of philosophy or metaphysics. He interpreted and set forth His ways in precepts, principles and example. His mind concerning prayer is seen in every command to pray, in every law of prayer, in every promise concerning prayer and every example of answered prayer. Every part of the whole, but every subject of scripture has its ends and complete expression, and in the conversion of Saul or Tarsus there is unique revelation of the mind of God concerning prayer.

There are three persons in that incidence of prayer. There is the man who pray, the God who heard, and the man through whom the prayer came. God is the centre. It is to Him prayer is made. Through Him prayer is interpreted, and by Him prayer is answered.

God speaks of prayer in terms of wonder. "Behold, he prayeth (Acts 9:11). The language is that of humanity, but it is the only speech man knows, and however inadequate it may be, it stands for corresponding reality in God. Can God wonder? Can there be in Him element of surprise and amazement? That is how God speaks, and to Him there is nothing more gloriously wonderful than prayer. It would seem as if the biggest creature in God's universe is a man who prays.

There is only one thing more amazing, and that I, that man knowing all these facts and refuse to pray. In the estimate of God, prayer is more wonderful than all the wonders of the Heavens, more glorious than all the mysteries of the Earth, more mightily than all the forces of creation. God interprets prayer as a sign of all that happened to Saul at Tarsus on the Damascus road. The event is variously expressed. To the churches of Judea it was a conversion that turned their arch-persecutor into a preacher. This is how Paul the Apostle states it in His writing to the Galatians: "Afterwards, I came into the regions of Syria and Cilicia; and was unknown by face into the churches of Judea which were in Christ, but they had heard only, that he which persecuted us in times past now preacheth the faith which once he destroyed. And they glorified God in me." (Gal. 1:21-24).

That is a conversation that was the result of an experience. What is the experience? Paul says that in the experience it pleased God to reveal His Son in Him. That is what the Damascus road experience meant to him. When God speaks of it He sums it all up in the words, "Behold, he prayeth, "That is what it meant to God, and that is what it always means to Him. Prayer is the symbol and proof and gauge of grace. All that happens in the converting work of grace, whereby we receive the adoption of sons. Therefore, being sons/daughters, we begin to pray. Prayer is the priviledge of sons/daughters and the test of sonship. It would seem as if God divided all men into the simple classification of those who pray and those who do not. It is a very simple test, but it is decisive, and divisive. There is joy in the heart of God the Father when His children begin to pray. He answers joyously. The answering hand of God waits for the lifted hands of man, and the heart that answers always transcends the heart that cries. God's servants are partners with Him in the Ministry of prayer. That is the mystery of spiritual cooperation! The Lord goes before the man He sends. Saul was prepared and waiting for the man he had already seen in a vision of God! Ananias found Saul prepared and waiting.

Prayer made all the difference to Saul of Tarsus, and it always makes all the difference. It brought a new assurance of God, a new confirmation of faith, a new fellowship of the people of God, a new experience of healing, a new vocation, a new inheritance, a new anointing, a new power. Prayer changes things. Prayer makes all things possible for it links the praying soul to the Omnipotence of God. Do we pray? Do we pray in our prayer? Does God put His seal on our prayers? Lord teach us to pray! Really our Heavenly Father wants to be taken into all the secret longings and desires of our Heart. He wants no desire hidden from Him but every desire turned into prayer. His word says in Phiilpians 4:6-7: "Be careful for nothing; but in everything by prayer and supplication with thanksgiving let your request be made known unto God. And the peace of God, which passeth all understandings, shall keep your hearts and minds through Christ Jesus."

Here is the cure for worry, anxious care, fretting, harassed faces and troubled hearts that comes from frustrated desires. Troubled uncertainty about the future can all be done away with if you will come to God and ask Him frankly and boldly for everything you want and stay there until He answer.

Prayer is the simplest form of speech that infant lips can try. Prayer is the sublimest stains that reach the Majesty on high. Prayer is Christians vital death, the Christians native air, his watchword at the gate of wealth. He enters heaven with prayer. R.H.531

Keeping On In Prayer

The prayer in life of Jesus awoke within His disciples a desire to be able to pray, and when they wanted to pray they found they did not know how! Then they asked Him in Luke 11:1: "And it came to pass, that, as he was praying in a certain place, when he ceased, one of His disciples said unto Him, LORD, TEACH US TO PRAY, as John also taught his disciples."

There was nothing extra-ordinary in the prayer of Jesus. But to hear Jesus pray would carry one, surely, into the very Holy of Holies! Can you imagine the groaning, the tears, the happy, child- like faith, the urgency with which Jesus prayed? How the disciples marveled and grew hungry- hearted as they heard Jesus prayed!

And when Jesus closed His prayer and looked up, one of the disciples, moved so deeply by hearing Jesus pray, said, "Lord teach us how to pray, as John also taught his disciples." John the Baptist had taught his disciples to pray. What a lesson for preachers and pastors! We should teach people how to pray. Christians do not automatically become great men and women of prayer just as soon as they are born again. Prayer is an art that requires teaching. Every pastors and teacher should set himself to training people in Christ – like prayer. So these disciples asked Jesus, "Lord teach us to pray." Christian should study how to pray. They should ask God to teach them to pray. They should train themselves in Christ-like prayer. Preponderance passage in Luke 11:2-13 was given by Jesus in response to this earnest request that He teaches His disciples to pray. Let us study these verses carefully. Let us learn to pray as Jesus Christ taught His disciples to pray. We should learn to pray in the spirit with which they prayed. We should pray for the same kind of things for which they asked. And we should pray with assurance and according to the will of God. We should get our prayers answered as they did.

To be able to get the result the disciples got; the first thing is to come with the same hungry heart the disciples had and pray the same prayer. My suggestion is that you should stop now, before you proceed to read the rest that is search your heart in a moment. Then can you pray the prayer of this hungry hearted disciples? If you can, then bow your heart before the Almighty God and earnestly, sincerely pray this prayer; "LORD TEACH ME TO PRAY."

Let us look to Christ as He teaches us through the scripture.

Jesus Prayer Principles

Lord Jesus gave a model for prayer, which multitudes call "The Lord's prayer" Let us learn to pray as Jesus taught His disciples to pray:

> "And He said unto them, when ye pray, say, Our Father which art in Heaven, Hallowed be thy name. Thy kingdom come. Thy will be done, as in Heaven, so in Earth. Give us this day our daily bread. And forgive us our sins; for we also forgive every one that is indebted to us. And lead us not into temptation; but deliver us from evils" (Luke 11:2,3,& 4).

This prayer is simple and universal in its usefulness. Every Christian from the most ignorant child to the most profound scholar can approach God, saying:

"Our Father which art in Heaven"
Everyone should approach reverently.

"Hallowed be thy name."

And all of us alike ought to pray for the Lord's return and His Kingdom on the Earth. How many times the saints of God have uttered these words.

"Thy Kingdom come. Thy will be done on Earth as it is in Heaven," Without realizing that thus we are to pray regularly for the return of Christ. That is blessed hope of every believers (Titus 2:13) John the beloved said, "Even so, come, Lord Jesus." (Rev. 22:20). It is worthy to note that this prayer is for common, universal needs of God's people.

"Give us day by day our daily bread."
We have a right to pray for our daily needs. Foods, clothes, shelter, a job, physical necessities are included in God's will for believers. You may not always get what you want but you ought to get all you need.

As a child confidently comes to the father or mother for food, so any genuine believer ought to come to God for daily needs. God is the maker of this world; and "Every good gift and every perfect gift is from above and cometh down from the father of lights." (James 1:17). The God who fed Elijah by ravens, and made the meal and the oil last all along for the widow and her son and the prophet of God (I Kings 17:2-16) and the hand that fed five thousand people with five loaves and two fishes, can still feed the saints of God and supply their needs.

God is our father. All the Heaven and the Earth are His and He will as gladly clothe His children as He does the lilies of the field. He will gladly feed His beloved as He does the fowls of the air. We are encouraged to pray today for today's bread. Tomorrow we need to pray again for tomorrow's bread.

"And forgive us our sins, as we forgive those who sin against us."
Every Christian needs to pray that prayer every day. We are saved yet according to the teaching of our Lord; we should come to God and get all the hindrance removed. By confessing our sins, we are cleansed and forgiven, as is faithfully promised in (I John 1:9). And when we come to God for daily cleansing and forgiveness, let us remember to forgive others.

I know that when one turn to Christ for salvation and depend upon Him in simple faith, he gets all his sins forgiven. All these sins have been laid upon Jesus Christ, who paid for them. The one who trust in Christ has everlasting life and never will come unto condemnation but is passed from death unto life (John 5:25). But after I am already a child of God, my common compromise, double tongue, and divided loyalty among others grieve God and must be dealt with, because they break God's heart, can hinder our fellowship, can grieve the Holy Spirit, can ruin my testimonies and my happiness. Daily, every believer needs His touch of sanctification. And one sure token of this is our willingness and gladness to forgive all those who sinned against us. This scripture could be linked with Matthew 5:7 that says: "Blessed are the merciful: for they shall obtain mercy". Let us learn this secret of daily conquering prayer – 'forgive and be forgiven' every day.

"And lead us not into temptation, but deliver us from evil." Every believer needs daily leading. We should daily ask for divine guidance to keep us out of temptation. King David in Psalm 23:3 said, "He leadeth me in the path of righteousness for His name's sake." We must daily tell our Father in heaven to keep us from the hands of the evil one. Prayer is a mighty weapon against temptation. Daily let us call on God for bread, for forgiveness, for guidance, for protection from sin and temptation of Satan.

This is the common school of prayer, the primary class of Christ school in prayer. Every believer should learn to pray in the Spirit the Lord's model prayer. Let us remember that God has far greater teaching on prayer than our personal needs.

Prayer Learned By Praying

There is no way to learn to pray except by praying. No reasoned philosophy of prayer ever taught anyone to pray. The subject is beset with problems, but there are no problems of prayer to the man who prays. They are all met in the fact of an answered prayer and joy of fellowship with God. We know not what we should pray for as we ought, and it prayer waits for understanding it will never begin. We must live by faith. We walk by faith. Edison once wrote: "We don't know the millionth part of one percent about anything. We don't know what water is. We don't know what light is. We don't know what gravitation is. We don't know what enable us to keep our feet when we stand up. We don't know what electricity is. We don't know what heat is. We don't know anything about magnetism. We have a lot of hypothesis about these things, but that is all. But we do not allow our ignorance about all these things to deprive us of their use." We discover by using. We learn by practice. Though a man may have sail knowledge about prayer, and though he understands all the mysteries about prayer, unless he prays he will never learn to pray.

There have been people that are mighty in prayer; they learned to pray. There was a period in their lives when they were as others in the matter of prayer, but they became mighty with God and prevailed. In every instance there was a crisis of grace, but it was in the discipline of grace that they discovered the secret power. They were known as men of God, because they were men of prayer. Some of them were re-named, like Jacob, Simon and Saul, they were called "Praying John" "Praying Mary" "Praying Hyde" our Redeemed fathers were mighty in prayer. They shook gates of hell by prayer. They opened the windows of heaven by prayer. How did they learn to pray? They learned to pray by being much in prayer. They did not talk about prayer, they did not argue about the mode of prayer; they just prayer.

Apprenticeship In Prayer

Prayer touches infinite extremes. It is so simple that a little child can pray, and it is so difficult that none but a child-like-heart can pray. The song in our Hymn says:

Prayer is the simplest form of speech
That infant lip can try
Prayer is the sublimnest strains that reach
The Majesty on High.

That is gloriously true. A cry brings God, a cry is mightier than the polished phrase. The Pharisees prayed within himself, to satisfy himself his prayer revolves on tubs of vanity of his own mind and heart. The Publican cried and was heard. It is not an emergency way out for believer we are talking about, but the sustained habit experience of the man of prayer. Such prayer comes by training. And there is no discipline, so tasking and exalting as this. But to pray as God would have us pray is the greatest achievement on the earth.

A life of prayer is costly. It takes time. Hurried prayer, muttered lullabies and daily tautology can never produce souls mighty in prayer. Learners give hours regularly every day that they may become proficient in its art and mechanism. Our Lord rose before day break that He might pray, and frequently He spent all night in prayers. All praying saints have spent hours every day in prayer. In these days of increase in activities and programmes in Christendom, no time is left to pray; but without time and even a lot of it, we may never learn to pray.

It ought to be possible to give God one hour of every twenty four all to Himself. Let us start the discipline of training in prayer by setting apart a fixed time every day for the practice of prayer. We must set our heart to learn how to pray as much as God is willing also to TEACH US TO PRAY.

The Person In Prayer

It is not other people's prayer that makes the man of prayer. I have heard people demanding for prayer support. As much as this is good, it is not the best. All true prayer, the prayer that prevails, is personal, intimate and original. Knowing this will make you a manifestor in the Kingdom of God on the earth. Hannah protested that she has poured out her soul to God. That is prayer.

The secret of Elijah's power in prayer was that he "Prayed fervently" His whole personality was in his prayer. That was the reason he went round for three and half years with the key of heaven in his pocket! He announced to the king "As the Lord God of Israel liveth, before whom I stand, there shall not be dew nor rain these years, but according to my word"(I Kings 17:1).

When Elijah was about to go to Heaven, Elisha with a boldness and heart purpose that defied Elijah, abruptly dismissed every suggestion of unbelief and seemed almost to demand of God instead of pleading (II Kings 2:1-4).

Time will fail us to list all the personalities involved in personal intimate prayer in the Bible. Read the story of how Moses prayed and God opened the Earth and swallowed up wicked men who challenged his leadership (Numbers 16:25-35).

Another accounts of how king Hezekiah prayed that heart-moving prayer of faith and how God heard, and "The angel of the Lord went forth, and smote in the camp of Assyrians a hundred and fourscore and five thousand, and when they arose early in the morning, behold, they were all dead corpses." (Isaiah 37).

This same Hezekiah was sick, and God Himself had told him to prepare to die, Hezekiah turned his face to the wall, ignored the warning of Isaiah,

God's prophet, and so prayed that God sent Isaiah back to tell him, "I have heard thy prayer, I have seen thy tears: behold, I will add unto thy days fifteen years" (Isaiah 38:1-5). Did ever a man pray so boldly! Then the sun turned ten degree backward on the sun dia (Isaiah 38; II Kings 19 & 20).

The only prayer that amount to anything is the "fervent" one not a formal routine, religion church service prayer. There are "many" prayers that avail to nothing as far as we can "Judge." Because, prayers are not measured by time or numbers but by intensity.

As we read through all these examples in the scriptures, any lowest heart must have seen that God intended us to be encouraged to pray "fervent, prevailing, initiative and original prayer as those personalities did.

Chapter 3
SECRECY
OF
PAPER

SECRECY OF PRAYER

Prayer is not a light undertaking. If prayer is the greatest achievement on earth, we can be sure that it will require discipline that corresponds to its power. The school of prayer has its condition and demands. It is a forbidden place to all those who are careless and not willing to take the cross of discipline. The reason so many people didn't pray is because of its cost.

The Secret Place

Our Lord has the authority to teach, and He himself is our example as well as instructor.

One of the first things He commands is that there shall be a place of prayer. It is quite true that the whole earth in the Lord's and that there is no place where prayer may not be heard. God wills that man should pray everywhere. Wherever we may be, He is right at hand, and afar off, and wherever there is a praying heart, the soul finds the sanctuary of God. No one would suggest that Jesus did not appreciate the sacredness of the earth, which He said was the footstool of God, but it was His habit to withdraw into solitary place to pray. He needed the fenced spaces of silence. To His disciples, He said in Matthew 6:5, 6:

"And when thou prayest, thou shall not be as the hypocrites are: for they love to pray standing in the synagogues and in the corners of the street, that they may be seen of men.

Verily I say unto you they have their reward, But thou, when thou prayest, enter into thy closet, and when thou has shut thy door, pray to thy Father which is in secret: and thy Father which seeth in secret shall reward thee openly."

Why does He insist upon this inner chamber and the closed door? The reason is that the first quality God requires in prayer is reality. Hypocrites never pray in secret. Prayers that are a pretence requires an audience. They are intended to be heard of men and they have their reward in still of phrasing, a show of earnestness, and a reputation for piety and spirituality. These things do not count with God. They cannot live in His presence. Prayer is between and individual and God alone. The normal Christian life is a life of regular, daily answer to prayer offered from the secret place. In the model prayer Jesus taught His disciples to pray daily for bread and expect to get it.

That is the way Jesus Himself lived – in daily unhindered communion with the Father, so that He could say to His Father and our Father, "I knew that thou hearest me always" (John 11:42). And all the teachings of the Lord Jesus about prayer show that we too have a normal, day-by-day unhindered intercourse with God, in the secret place, asking and receiving, seeking and finding, knocking and having – God open to us. He plainly said "Hitherto have ye asked nothing in my name; ask, and you shall receive, that your joy may be full" (John 16:24). When we are told in James 4:2, "that ye have not, because ye ask not, "it is proper to infer that God intended asking to be followed by having and that believer in the will of God can live daily in the fullness of joy of having his prayer answered at the secret place.

It is perfectly in order for an obedient child to look for food every day and get it, get all he wants, and eat until he is perfectly satisfied. The Saviour Himself said, "If ye then, being evil, know how to give good gifts unto your children how much more shall your Father which is in heaven give good things unto them that ask him? (Matthew 7:11).

A good depositor whose account is in good condition normally has every cheque he draws honoured by bank. Then why cannot a child of God day by day draw on the bank of Heaven, have his prayers answered as a matter of course, as a daily business? When a Christian fails to have his prayers cheque cashed, he should be aware that something is wrong at the secret place.

When I turn the tap in kitchen or bathroom, I expect water to pour forth every time. If I turn it and water does not come, I would know that something radically was wrong and I would set out to find out why the water did not run. If I press a light switch and the light does not shine, or if I plug in an electric radio and there is no power, I know that something is wrong, truly wrong, that the connection with the power house is broken: and I will set out to find what is wrong and also to rectify it. Just like this every believer ought to be in daily communion with God and to live the joyful life of answered prayer.

The neglect of secret place is the reason for emptiness, sorrow, powerlessness, poverty, bondage and a hosts of unpalatable experience that many believers are exposed to in our day; let us get back to the secret place David said in Psalm 91:1

"He that dwelleth in the secret place of the Most High shall abide under the shadow of the Almighty."

The Silent Spaces Of the Heart

The believer's heart needs its silent spaces. It is in them we learn to pray alone, shut in with God. Our Lord bids us pray to our Father which is in secret, and seeth in secret. There is no test like SOLITUDE. Hearts must be pure and hands clean that dare shut the door and be alone with God. It will revolutionize the lives of most men if they were shut in with God in some secret place for have an hour a day (Psalm 24:3-6).

For such praying all the faculties of the heart need to be awaken and alert. When our Lord took Peter, James and John with Him to the secret place of prayer, they were heavy with sleep. It was the same Mount of Glory and the Garden of Agony, and it was not until they were fully awake that they saw the glory or realize the anguish. There are some silent places of rare wisdom where men may not talk but they find it impossible to sleep. Mourning is not meditation, and drowsy repose is not praying. The secret place of prayer calls for every faculty of mind and heart.

"Bless the Lord, O my soul; And all that is within me, Bless His Holy Name." (Psalm 103:1)

As for praise, so for prayer – the whole being is to be involved. There is a vital difference between private and corporate prayer. Each kind of prayer brings blessings after its kind. Corporate prayer is less exacting. There is a sense of fellowship that gives courage and inspires expression. Guided prayer is companionable, but it has a tendency to do its thinking by proxy. In private prayer the soul stands naked and alone in the presence of God. Thought is personal, prayer is original, motive is challenged Corporate prayer gives a spirit of fellowship private prayer disciplines personality. Who can measure the influence of an hour a day spent alone with God?

The Mountain of the Lord

The way into the Holy presence is not a thoroughfare. The inner-chamber into which a man goes is his own, but it is the presence of God that makes it a Holy Place. To a secular mind there would be no presence. It is the seeking soul that finds. There are some people to whom no audience is given. There are people who cannot pray James says of some men that they need not think they can receive anything of the Lord. Even before Christ taught men to pray, the Psalmist declare, "If I regard iniquity in my heart, the Lord will not hear." (Psalm 66:18). The judgement seat of God is in the inner chamber, but the throne of Grace is there also, or none would ever dare to enter in. Forgotten sins start into life and hidden things or agenda stand naked and open before Him with whom we have to do. All who would enter the Holy presence and live, must have a sincere desire for God and a conscience set on dwelling in the light.

Our Lord laid emphasis upon the forgiven spirit. The one thing above all things that bolts and bars the way into the presence chamber of prayer is unwillingness to forgive from the heart. No gift can be accepted of God until reconciliation has been made. "If therefore thou bring thy gift to the altar, and there rememberest that thy brother hath ought against thee, leave there thy gift before the altar, and go thy way, first be reconciled to thy brother, and then come and offer thy gift." (Matthew 5:23-24)

Again when Jesus started the law of faith in relation to prayer, He said: "Therefore, I say unto you, what things whatsoever ye desire, when ye pray, believe that ye have receive them, and ye shall have them. And whenever ye stand praying, forgive, if ye have ought against any one, that your father also which is in heaven may forgive you your trespasses, but if ye do not forgive, neither will your father which is in heaven forgive your trespasses" (Mark 11:24-26).

Why did he lay such emphasis upon forgiveness? It is for the same reason that the law and the prophets place the emphasis upon righteousness. All who will come to the Holy one must be Holy, and whoever will come to the God of mercy, must be merciful. The petitioner for the grace must believe in grace.

Thine Inner Room

Let no one be discouraged from making a beginning. Schools are graded to the capacity of the learners. The great believer who became mighty in prayer and rejoiced to spent three and four hours a day alone with God, were once beginners. They went from strength to strength. For our consolation let remember that it is our own inner room we enter, and the God who is there is our Father. The story was told of a little girl who went to the bedroom of a man of God. She prattled bitterly over all the wonders of her child world, but the man of God asked if her father was up, she looked radiantly and reverently into the eyes of this man of God and said "Oh, my daddy always talk with God in the drawing room before breakfast."

Happy father! Happy child! Happy God!.

The Closed Door

"And when thou prayest, thou shall not be as the hypocrites are: for they love to pray stnding in the synagogues and in the corners of the streets, that they may be seen of men. Verily I say unto you, they have received their reward.

But thou, when thou prayest, enter into thy closet, and when thou hast shut thy door, pray to thy Father which is in secret; and thy Father which seeth in secret shall reward thee openly." (Matthew 6:5-6).

There are two difficulties awaiting us at the threshold of this command. One is that many have no inner chamber.

There is no place in their lives for privacy. They have no room that is not shared, and if they could find room they have no leisure.

The closed may neither shut out nor shut in. The wireless has made us familiar with the fact that neither bolted doors nor shuttered windows can secure privacy. But thought is more subtle than sound, and Satan is more cunning than the wireless expert. The believers who are into the practice of private prayer can bear witness of the adversaries that keep watch at the door of the heart's inner chamber.

Creating a Speech Atmosphere

My goal here is not to instruct, but to suggest. Manuals of devotion have usually been to me depressing rather than helpful – they are either too mechanical, scanty or too exacting. Some discourage rather than inspire. I want to write frankly, as a person. All my life I have wanted to learn to pray. In my zeal I have experimented and explored in likely and unlikely ways in the school/ study of prayer, and without pose or pride I want in all meekness and humility to tell you what I have learned. I speak for myself. I judge no man's methods criticize no man's counsel, challenge no man's experience or exposure. I speak with utmost simplicity, and you must judge what I say.

Let us begin with difficulty of privacy. There are tens of thousands of Christ's disciples who have no room to which they can retire for private prayer. They live with other people, sleep with other people, work with other people. They cannot escape from people. This is a reason why the door of the house of God should never be closed. Many houses of prayer were locked and bolted, back and front seven days in a week except on one or two evening for service of one or two hours. The secret place of prayer should be part of daily life, a part of the daily dwelling place.

Some place must be found that shall be a trashing place with God. A hungry heart will find a way. In the open air or in some scheduled corner, some inner sanctuary will be found. If this advantage is impossible, the believer must make an open space into which it can withdraw, even in the presence of others, and be alone with God; but the "inner chamber" is an unspeakable boon. Happily, God wills that men should pray everywhere, but the place of His glory is in the SOLITUDES, where He hides us in the cleft of the rock, and talks with man face to face as a man talks with his friend.

To Secure the Closed Door

How is it possible to keep the world from coming in and the mind from staying out? Concentration on any subjects is a severe strain upon the mind, and nowhere is it so difficult as in the place of and practice of private prayer.

An enemy is there to raise bodies, excite conscience, peg memory and direct invaders of sacred hours. Some simple device will usually secure the secret place from intrusion a man of God said "I hang a card outside my door when

I wish to be along." As good as this could be it could only keep people out, it is useless against the distractions of the mind, and a body may just as well be roaming at large with shut wandering mind. How can the door be so shut as to keep out the things that divert and distract? Attention is an act of the will.

Concentration is sustained attention upon a specific object. The will can be disciplined and the power of concentration developed. By patience and discipline, the mind is trained. God is in secret. Our first act is to affirm the fact of the Holy presence. Call every faculty of mind and body to remembrance recognition and realization of the God that is in secret and seeth in secret, hold the mind to this fact. Tolerate no distraction, allow no diversion, and indulge to dissipation. Every faculty must be alert. The Apostles in the Holy Mount, it was said they were heavy with sleep, but when they were fully awake they saw the glory. Dreaming is not meditation, dozing is not thinking. Moping is not praying. Prayer in the secret place demand all one's faculty at its best.

Our Lord gave His disciples a form and order of prayer, and does not begin with either song or supplication, but with contemplation and deep thought of God:

Our Father, which art in Heaven, Hallowed be thy Name (Matthew 6:9).

It is in this way all the great prayers of the Bible begin. That is how I find it helpful to begin. I think in adoring love and wonder of His character and attributes, of His majesty and might, of His grace and glory. Musing kindles the fire, and the flame become "a wall of fire round about" which keeps beasts and intruders at a safe distance. That is why I so often find that prayer in the secret place begins with Adoration and abounds in glory and thanksgiving. It is there the transfigured Lord is seen.

Chapter 4

GOD'S PRAYER MANUAL

GOD'S PRAYER MANUAL

The WORD of God quickens the heart and instructs it in prayer. The Psalmist speaks for all who pray when he acknowledge the seasons when his souls could not find its wings: "My soul cleaveth unto dust, quicken thou me according to thy word." It is always to the word of God he turns for quickening and instruction. Apostle Paul also links together the word of God and prayer. "And take ... the sword of the spirit which is the word of God; praying always with all prayer and supplication in the spirit and watching there into with all perseverance and supplication; and for me." (Ephesians 6:17-19). Watching where and whereat? Watching with all perseverance! That is surely with diligence and patience, alertness and reverence. We must search the word that we may know how to pray. "God is a Spirit, and they that worship Him must worship Him in spirit and in truth." (John 4:24).

Word Of God In Prayer

I never take any book but the Bible and my prayer diary into the secret place. The word of God is my prayer book. I seek no external aid to devotion materials. I have no altar but the one within my heart. Other believers may have other ways. Most people have some devotional materials, (daily this or that) but I do not take even hymn book: I am more on the devotional use of Bible and I feed upon it by searching its truth, appropriating its affirmation, and turning its psalms and prayers into personal thanksgiving and supplication. The word is more to me than my necessary food. It thrills and moves me with tremendous power.

The word of God instructs us how to pray. The posture of the body must be determined by conditions of health and comforts. Kneeling down may not be compulsory, we can also stand up, or sit down while praying but whatever the posture we assume we must not be engaged in self-deceit in His presence. Sleeping in the secret place is a false life. Prayer is more than asking, but even our asking should be instructed under the direction of the Holy Spirit. The Bible said in Romans 8:26:

"Likewise the spirit also helpeth our infirmities; for we know not what we should pray for as we ought; but the spirit itself maketh intercession for us with grooming which cannot be uttered." I find it good to rehearse and review my daily life in the Holy presence. It is there I make my plans. God guides with His eyes, and eyes speak best in the place of secret communion. It is there we are assured of His will and are made to understand His ways.

It is the place of intercession. That is the place where we can talk freely with God about other people. The family, the church, the business, the friendships, the state, the nation, the world are all subjects of earnest and private prayer. Keep a prayer list of people for whom you pray. It is not necessary to tell anyone else the things you tell God. The Father sees in secret; leave it to Him to make it known.

We pray as sons and daughter in the Father's house. He knows our need better than we can tell Him, and He is able to do exceeding abundantly above all we ask or think, therefore ask in confidence, not in doubt. It is in the secret place we learn that silence is the best speech and listening is the best part of praying. Those who speak are heard, and those who listen hear. This is said about Jesus: "And in the morning, rising up a great while before day. He went out, and departed into a solitary place and there, he prayed." (Matthew 1:35).

It Helps Devotion

It must be remembered that I do not judge any man in the method of devotion. I speak only of myself and my little walking experience with God. The practice of private prayer is so difficult to maintain, that extra aid apart from the manual of God will be a hindrance rather than a help. Many find help in book of devotion; "daily this and daily that." Although this has been to ten thousands who have sought to know how to pray. It may be a "confession of shame, but I do not want any of them in the inner chamber." I can appreciate them, more or less, elsewhere, but surely not here.

There are two mistakes to be avoided one is emotional unreality and the other is intellectual pre-occupation. An earnest believer whose religious enthusiasm found expression in service to God, the church and humanity was convicted of prayerlessness. He earnestly resolved to spend half an hour everyday in personal prayer. At the end of a month he gave it up, because he could not endure the sense of unreality. There was not only no sense of His presence, but there was a very real consciousness of an absence. There can be no experience of heart speech and spiritual fellowship without a consciousness of His presence. The heart cannot keep up an emotional make-believe day after day. The mind cannot live in a vacuum. The father is in secret, but is the glory of His presence that makes up the sanctuary. There must be truth as well as the Holy Spirit in all worship, and nowhere is the combination more necessary than in the secret place of prayer.

Altar fires are kindled and quickened by the truth and the Holy Spirit, but this must get to the altar. Devotional studies do not necessarily lead to devotion. There may be a pre-occupation with truth that becomes an obsession. The study of experimental truth may never become experience and experiences of others become a snare. Our Lord reproached the religious teachers of His day because this misuse of the scripture blinded their minds. Stepping-stones may become slipping- stones, and even a corner-stone may become a stumbling block. To this end, use your own productive methods.

Devotional Use Of The Bible

Do you still have a Bible you can take to the Holy Place? Many believers have substituted for the Bible for other devotional books, and there is no book on the earth that shows the truth; truth is essential to man and God. If we are to worship Him, we must do this in spirit and in truth. The scripture are still the "Living and sovereign word of God." Jesus took the Bible at its face value, and in it He found His gospel, on it He fed His spirit and in all the great crisis of His life relied upon its truth. We His disciple must be contented to be like our master.

The Word Empowered Prayers

The word of God is like God's world: It is interesting and all wonderful, but there are places to which we go often in thought and affection if not in actual visit; beauty-stops of which we never tire, sacred places of hallowed association. So there are pages of the Bible that wear thin and some that are stained with tears. There are favourite books that register the pilgrimage of the believer. I love the Psalms 37, 46, 116 and many more besides. Sometimes I read through the Psalms, and then return for meditation to a few verses that have appealed to me. Many time I have countered "fret" with "TRUST" committed my way unto the Lord, and hummed and pray through the matchless words, "O rest in the Lord and wait patiently for Him," and my soul rejoices in the assurance that if I delight myself in the Lord. He will give me the desire of my heart. It is great to take the Lord's own words and speak them in praise and plead them in prayer.

What can we do against a changing earth, hurting mountains and ranging storm God is our refuge. The refuge is for safety and when we are totally helpless. "Eternal God is thy refuge, and underneath are the everlasting arms." Always underneath! Always lower than our deepest depth! God is also our strength. There are demands for which we have no might and enemies against whom we have not strength." He gives power to the faint and to them that have no might, He increaseth strength. As we remind God His Holy words, our faith rejoices in the assurance of His Strength. "Te Lord of Hosts is with me, and the God of Jacob is my refuge."

I can face the day when I have beheld His glory, and said Amen. Hellelujah! In His presence, at night I can see the vision of ultimate triumph and rest my heart in His peace. And I can say like King David: "Return unto thy rest, O my soul, for the Lord hath dealth bountifully with thee. For thou has delivered my soul from death, mine eyes from tears, and my feet from falling. I will walk before the Lord in the land of the living"

There is a closed connection between the word of God and prayer (Prov. 28:9) says. The prayer of the one that turns his heart away from hearing the law, is abomination. How could the one who have his heart turn away from the word, please God in prayer? What claim could such and unspiritual heart, such and alienated child, have on God in prayer all the promises in the Bible concerning answers to prayer involve in some way a heart that is eager to find the will of God in the word of His. In John 15:7 Jesus promised, "If ye abide in me, and my words abide in you, ye shall ask what ye will, and it shall be done unto you." And how can a Christian who does not know the heart of God ask Him in prayer. Every believer, then, should long for and earnestly seek a delightful familiarity, an unceasing interest in the word of God. If you surrender yourself, and do not rush, but meditate on the word of God, you will find prayer forming in your heart. It is a prayer inspired by the Holy Spirit, a prayer that God will be pleased to hear and answer.

A daily quiet time of reading the word of God, memorizing it, subjecting oneself to the searching, probing, judging, purifying action of God's word will mean rich prosperity in your prayer life. But "he that turneth away ear from hearing the law, even his prayer shall be abomination."

Chapter 5

POWER FOR PREVAILING PRAYER

POWER FOR PREVAILING PRAYER

What then is the power for prevailing prayer? How do we enforce the divine authority to avail in praying? Let see me devote this chapter to consider this vital topic.

Praying In His Name

The power of His name we can best wield in prayer. All His divine promises are connected to the uses of the mighty name of Jesus.

The most incredible things promised are linked to prayer. The word of God abounds in promises and examples. Deliverance and help, guidance and grace were assured to those who called upon God and committed their way unto Him. Nothing was too hard for the Lord, and nothing was impossible to those who prayed. Some of the passages in the Old Testaments are overwhelming in their challenges to prayer. Here is one:

"Thus said the Lord, the Holy One of Israel, and His maker: Ask me of the things that are to come concerning my sons, and concerning the work of my hands, command ye me." (Isaiah 45:11).

Prayer passes from entreaty to command. There is no limit to the possibility of prayer, the examples and demonstrations in the word of God confirms and attests to these unlimited promises.

Our Lord speaks with the same clear speech. His word is "Ask and it shall be given unto you; seek and ye shall find, knock and it shall be open unto you; for everyone that asked received, and he the seeketh findeth: and to him that knocketh it shall it shall be opened. (Matthew 7:7-8). He gave prayer a new basis, a new confidence and a new range. "If ye, then, being evil, know how to give good gifts unto your children, how much more shall your heavenly father which is in heaven give good things to them that ask Him" (Matt. 7:11). He ask us to pray for whatever we desire. "Therefore, I say unto you WHAT THING SO EVER YE DESIRE, when ye pray, believe that ye receive them, and ye shall have them." (Mark 11:24). Anything in the world you want, even to the casting of a mountain into the sea, is included in the boundaries of legitimate, normal prayer for a Christian! The condition of faith is given, to be sure. We are not here discussing the conditions but calling your attention to the wonderful, unlimited invitation to pray for the things your heart desires, whatever they may be.

The gospel of John 15:7 taught us this same thing, where Jesus said, if ye abide in me, and my word abides in you, ye shall ASK WHAT YE WILL, and it shall be done unto you." Psalm 37:4 also said, "Delight thyself also in the Lord; and he shall give thee THE DESIRES OF THINE HEART." A believer's prayer should coincide with the desire of his heart. Whatever the heart desires, the Christian should ask for.

ANYTHING may be requested by one of God's children in prayer, according to the sweet invitation of the savior Himself. In John 14:13-14. Jesus said, "AND WHATSOEVER ye shall ask in my name, that will I do, that the father may be glorifies in the Son. If ye shall ASK ANYTHING in my name, I will do it" WHATSOEVER, means anything in the world. And then Jesus knowing the unbelief people hearts, simply said "Anything you ask in my name I will do it." Believers ought to ask for anything, literary anything. They want from God.

Many people set limited opinions about the proper manner of prayer, so they have most limited views of the proper subject of prayer. Some think it is wrong to ask for rain, for jobs, for money, or for particular, definite daily bread, despite the Saviour's model prayer in Gospel of Matthew.

Likewise, other people think that on every great matter it is proper to pray, but on small matters it would not be right to take God's time nor ask for His help. But Christians need to break away from these traditional limitations on prayer and learn from the Bible that a child of God has a right to pray about anything and everything in the name of Jesus.

Just imagine that the Lord Jesus should knock at the door of your house and say, "I have come to supply your needs, to supply every legitimate wants, to make you fully happy." I think you would surely make your request known and tell Him anything you needed or wanted. Well that is exactly what He says for you to do. It is a shameful and wicked to set our hearts on anything that we cannot honestly talk to God about. But anything we have a right to work for, anything we have a right to want, anything we have a right to buy or plan about, that we have a right to pray for, ask for anything you want in His name.

Whatsover Ye Shall Ask In My Name

The promises of prayer reach climax in the upper room in that memorable night of revelation. He declared Himself to be the basis of prayer. They were to pray in a new way. They were to pray in His name, and they will be heard for His sake. Of course the Bible do not say we are to simply add unto our prayer the label "We ask in Jesus name." But if we are in full surrender to the will of God, and if we have his words abiding in us so that we know that perfect will of God, then manifestly it will be easy to get the things we want in His

The upper room fellowship was a piece of submission and total surrender for the disciple. They gather up and complete the whole revelation of the scriptures, and enlarge and certify the promises of God. Those Holy and sacred promises are as follows:

> "And whatsoever ye shall ask in my name, that will I do, that the father may be glorified in the son. If ye shall ask anything in my name, I will do it." (John 14:13-14).

> "If ye abide in me, and my words abide in you, ye shall ask what ye will, and it shall be done unto you." (John 15:1).

"Ye have not chosen me, but I have chosen you, and ordained you, that ye should go and bring forth fruit, and that your fruit should remain; that whatsoever ye shall ask of the father in my name, he may give it to you." (John 15:16).

"And ye now therefore have sorrow; but I will see you again, and your heart shall rejoice, and your joy no man take from you. And in that day ye shall ask me nothing (No question).

Verily, I say unto you, whatsoever ye shall ask the father in my name, he will give it to you. Hitherto have ye asked nothing in my name, ask and ye shall receive, that your joy may be full" (John 16:22-26).

What extraordinary promises these are to pray in that name of Lord Jesus Christ. Prayer reaches its highest level when offered in the name that is above every other name. For it lifts person in prayer into unity and identify with Christ.

We are to get all things by asking in His name this abound in universal and unconditional terms. But you may say the way for a farmer to grown a crop is to break his land, sow his seed, plow out the weeds. In other words, the way to have a crop would be by diligent and intelligent work. But I have seen some farmers who worked hard and intelligently, then there was no rain and the made no harvest or rather poor harvest! Or storms beat down the maize or the millet before it could be harvested. Or worms ruined the cotton. So human wisdom and human toiling cannot be relied upon. No, a believer is not to depend upon his/her own toil nor his/her own planning but he is not to ask of God in the name of Jesus.

In The Name of Jesus Christ

Our Lord never explained what was meant by praying in His name. The meaning was plain enough to every believer. God was in His name. He had made them an elect people that they ought to be the interpreters, custodians, and witnesses of His name.

When our Lord speaks about praying in His name, it is deeper than mere adding "In Jesus name to our prayer or petitions. The name expresses personality, character, and being. The person is in the Name. Prayer in Christ's name is prayer according to the character of His mind, and according to the purpose of His will. To pray in the name of Christ is to pray as one who is at one with Christ, whose mind is the mind of Christ, whose desire are desires of Christ, and whose purpose is one with that of Christ.

Such correspondence and identification with Christ secure the balance and interpretation of the promises given to prayer. The absolute and unconditional promises find their relativity and condition in Him. Throughout the Bible, prayer was conditioned upon urgency, intensity and sincerity. God was found of men when they cried unto Him out of a great need, when they sought Him with all their heart, and when there was sincerity of purpose and motive. Men found that God required the truth in the innermost heart. And they were not heard if they regarded iniquity in their hearts, or come to him with insincere pretense upon their lips. Our Lord demanded importunity and a forgiveness spirit of all who prayed in the prayer in the name, all conditions are unified and simplified in Him. Sincerity is tested in the name.

Motive is judged in the name. Prayer is proved in the name. Prayer is sanctified in the name. And prayer is endorsed by the name when it is in harmony with the character, mind, desire and purpose of the name. That is why in John 15:7, Christ said, "if ye abide in me, and my words abide in you, ye shall ask what ye will, and it shall be done unto you."

I John 3:21-22 said "Beloved, if our heart condemn us not, then we have confidence towards God, and whatsoever we ask, we receive of Him, because we keep His commandments, and do those things that are pleasing in His sight. "Prayer offered in the name of Jesus are scrutinized and sanctified by His nature. His purpose and His will. They are endorsed by Him.

Various promises of the Lord are not a series of barricades, all of which we must climb over to get anything from God. Rather, they are different avenues of approach. If you cannot come through one, then God makes another for you. And it you do not know that you can ask in the name of Jesus, yet you have a right to come and say, "My Father."

Praying In The Spirit

Next is the prevailing power we wield when we pray in the Holy Ghost.

The WORK of the Holy Spirit is always in cooperation. He never work alone. He depends on human cooperation, for the meditation of His mind, the manifestation of His truth, and the effectual working of His will. He indwells the body of Christ, as Christ dwelt in the body prepared for Him by the Holy Spirit. Revelation came from the Spirit of truth as men of God were inspired by Him. The word is His, but the writing is with the hands of men. This two-fold action runs through the whole of redemption by Christ Jesus. Our Lord was born of a woman, but conceived by the Holy Spirit of God. He grew in stature and in knowledge in the house of Joseph, instructed and guided by the Holy Spirit. His teaching and ministry were in the power of the same spirit. He offered Himself without blemish unto God through the eternal spirit, and it was the spirit that raised up Christ from the dead. There is the same co-operation in all the experiences of salvation. There is always a human and divine factor. There is a two-fold witness, a two-fold leading, a two-fold work, and a two-fold intercession. We pray in the Spirit, and the spirit maketh intercession for us.

Fellowship Of The Spirit In Prayer

The Holy Spirit does nothing of Himself, neither does He do anything for Himself, His mission is to glorify

Christ, and all He does is based upon the finished work of Christ. He could not be sent until Jesus was glorified and in experience there can be no Pentecost until there is a coronation. The fellowship of the Spirit is prayer as set up in sequence in Romans 8:9-27. Those who pray in the Spirit must be in the Spirit, and if the Spirit of God is to make intercession for us, He must dwell in us. If we live after flesh we die, if we are led by the Spirit, and walk not after the flesh, but after the Spirit, then the Spirit dwells in us, lives through us, and work by us. Then it will come to pass that which is written, "And in like manner the Spirit also helpeth our infirmities: for we know not how to pray as we ought; but the Spirit Himself (that dwelleth in us) maketh intercession for us with groaning which cannot be uttered; and He that searcheth the hearts knoweth what is the mind of the Spirit, because He maketh intercession for the saint according to the will of God." He takes of the things of Christ and reveals them unto us. God knows the mind of the Spirit; as we pray in the Spirit, instructed and inspired by Him, and makes intercession for us in wordless intercession. That is the New Testament that prevails. As I live, yet not I; so I pray, yet not I. I pray in the spirit, and the Spirit Himself also maketh intercession.

Holy Spirit Helping Our Infirmities

The Holy Spirit instructs and inspires all true prayer. There is no truer word than that "we know not what we should pray for as we ought." There is no realm in which we so soon come to the end of what we know as in that of prayer. We cannot see deep enough or far enough to know what is our real need. Most people would like good health, home comfort, congenial conditions, happy friendship, a little more money and better success, but their request are never channeled through the Holy Spirit who knows the mind of Christ and the express will of God, and He teaches us how to pray and what to pray for.

The Holy Spirit creates the condition for prayer. We may ask amiss, not only in what we ask, but also in the reason or motive for asking. He sanctifies desire and directs in into the will of God, so that we desire what God wills to give. That is how it comes topass that if we delight ourselves in the Lord, we can be sure that he will give us the desire of our heart. We want what He wills. The Spirit brings to expression unutterable things of the heart. His groaning are before our praying, and our prayers are born of his travail. In Him is the supply of life a desire, wisdom, faith, intercession and power. He quickens desire, purifies motives, inspires confidence and assures faith.

Speaking In The Spirit

This is the inner meaning of prayer. It is more than asking, it is communion, fellowship, cooperation, identification with God the Father and Son by the Holy Spirit. Prayer is more than words, for it is mightiest when wordless. It is more than asking, for it reaches its highest glory when it adores and ask nothing. When a child entered his father's study and walked up to him at his desk, the father turned and asked, "What did you want, Uche?" "The little girl answered, "Nothing Daddy, I just came to be with you."

This mystery of the Spirit is the key to other mysteries. The secret of the Lord is made manifest to those who pray in fellowship of the Spirit. There are stages of prayer i.e. Primary, Secondary and Tertiary levels. In one stage we pray and ask for help. There is wonderful way in which He prays and we assent, and His praying is ours. He makes intercession within the Temple of our hearts, and our Lord ever lives to make intercession for us at the right hand of the Father. The Spirit within our Spirit prays, working in us to will and to do the will and good pleasure of our Father God. The assurance of answer to prayer comes from the Holy Spirit and He is the one that makes the prayer the mightiest force in the universe. The secret of it all is in Him. The power of it all is by Him. The joy of it all is with Him. The biggest thing God ever did for me was to teach me to pray in the Spirit.

"We are never really men of prayer in the best sense until we are filled with the Holy Spirit."

Praying With Faith

Faith is a certain conviction, an assurance, evidence that we will get the thing we hope for and ask for. By faith one sees the thing that is invisible. By faith one holds what is intangible. One who has faith has the substance of the thing hoped for and had the evidence of that which is not yet seen by human eye. What a blessed confidence and assurance of faith.

"Now faith is the substance of things hoped for; the evidence of things not seen". (Hebrews 11:1).

The word of God says in Hebrews 11:6 that: "But without faith it is impossible to please Him; for he that cometh to God must believe that He is, and that He is a rewarder of them that diligently seek Him."

You cannot come to God unless you believe that He is God that hear and answers prayer. Faith is the very first requirement for anyone who would do anything pleasing to God. Without faith you cannot pray an acceptable prayer. Without faith you will be far from victorious living. Therefore faith is the first demand or requirement from the one that prays.

It is the prerequisite for any meaningful prayer; the sole condition of salvation; and essential ingredients of a fruitful Spiritual life and the universal law of power. Faith is enough. Faith is all Jesus asks: "Ye believe in God, believe also in Me." When the ruler of synagogue was told that his daughter was dead, Jesus re-assured his faith, saying, "Fear not; only believe" and when the distraught father of the demonic boy cried out in despair, our Lord re-affirm him that "all things are possible to him that believeth." Without faith it is impossible to please God. Without faith man cannot do anything with God and God cannot do anything with man.

Faith Is A Command Duty

One early morning Jesus was walking from the little town where He spent the night to Jerusalem. Jesus caused the fig tree and it withered away. They returned in the night and the next morning the disciples saw the fig tree withered and were astonished. Jesus turned to them and commanded them, "Have faith in God!" (Mark 11:22).

And then the mountains could be removed and cast into the sea by faith, that they could have what things soever they desired if they believe. "Have faith in God" is a plain command. Believers are commanded to have, and can have faith.

Jesus said to Thomas, reach hither they finger, and behold my hands: and reach hither thy hand, and thrust it into my side, and be not faithless, but believing (John 20:27).

To every believer the Lord Jesus cries out, find out for yourselves the proof of God's promises. Give God a chance to prove Himself. "Be not faithless but believing."

You Can Get Anything By Faith

How marvelous is faith. The Bible says in Matthew 17:20: "If ye have faith as grain of mustard seed, ye shall say unto this mountain, remove hence to yonder place; and it shall be removed; and nothing shall be impossible to you."

Absolutely, "Nothing shall be impossible to you." Also the Lord said in Mark 9:23 "If thou can't believe all things are possible to him that believeth." And in Mark 11:24 He said: "Therefore I say unto you what things so ever ye desire, when ye pray, believe that ye received them and ye shall have them." We are given a clear and unconditional promise that "the prayer of faith shall save the sick; and the Lord shall raise him up." (James 5:15).

It is so clear that if you will believe God, you can have anything you ask. With faith, nothing in the earth or in heaven is impossible, and nothing is unattainable. That means one must have faith for each particular thing you want to have. Faith for salvation, healing, good home, job and deliverance to mention just few. One must be in harmony with God that he can base his request on a blessed promise or on the known will of God to get the prayer answered.

However, faith is not an evidence by which any poor wicked man have his own will irrespective of God's will of God to get the prayer answered.

However, faith is not evidence by which any poor wicked man have his own will irrespective of God's will. Nothing about prayer – Telephone to glory is ever intended for that ever attains. Faith is a grace, or a gift, by which, in a particular matter, one must ask for things in the will of God, and having a duly base confidence he may receive whatever he asks.

It is very important, for every believers to learn what faith factor is to prayer, to learn how to have it and how to suppress and forsake unbelief for a meaningful life of victorious faith.

Faith Is In His Word

We are told without missing word that, "Faith cometh by hearing and hearing by the Word of God." (Romans 10:17). Originally the word of God was principally obtained by hearing instead of reading. There were few copies of the word of God, all copied by hand. Most people could not read, so they got the word of God secondhand. So faith came by hearing that is, hearing the word of God. But the essential point is that faith principally comes by familiarity and have faith in God standing of the word of God. If you want to have faith in God, you must know His word. This is absolutely true, because faith is based upon God's promises. If God said He will do a thing, He will.

If God made a proposition, He will stick to it. God's guarantees are always fulfilled. But you will not know what God has promised unless you learn His word. So one who want to please God with a faith that gets prayer answered and collect for him all that God wishes to give them through your Bible. Read them with delight. Mark them for quick reference. Memorize them so that the blessed assurance of them may sink into your soul. Learn God's promises if you would come to depend upon Him. Then you should take these promises to heart. Take them as personal to yourself.

If God made a proposition, He will stick to it. God's guarantees are always fulfilled. But you will not know what God has promised unless you learn His word. So one who want to please God with a faith that gets prayer answered and collect for him all that God wishes to give him, should set out to find the blessed promises of God. Search for them through your Bible. Read them with delight Mark them for quick reference. Memorize them so that the blessed assurance of them may sink into your soul. Learn God's promises if you would come to depend upon Him. Then you should take these promises to heart. Take them as personal to yourself.

Search out the scriptures: meditate over them lovingly; pray for the Holy Spirit to help you understand them that you may get exactly what is the sense of God's promises and how they are to apply to you. Only as you get the exact meaning of God's promises can you know He has obligated Himself to do and what you can count on His doing. This comes through an understanding of the word of God. The Holy Spirit build faith in the heart by the means of God's word, particularly His blessed promises.

Prayer is not a way of taking from God things He does not want to give us. Rather, prayer is intended to find what in God's sweet will, then to ask for and receive all that God has for us. And what God has for us is so much richer and better happier than what we can desire in our will that there can be no comparison.

Praying in the will of God means bigger prayers, not smaller ones: bigger answer not small answer. Praying in God's will means not so much giving up so as to get. Let there be no mistake; real faith is exercised only in the will of God. God never gives faith for things contrary to His will. One way to grow great, robust faith is to act on God's promises. Put God to test. He will prove Himself, and you will have a stronger assurance than ever before that you can rely on God's faithfulness.

God Is Trust Worthy!

God will do what He promises! Anybody in the world should know that if he will only give God a chance to prove it. Take God at His words, risk Him, depend on Him, your answer will come and your faith will be encouraged. Faith is not feeling. Faith is acting on what God has said. Jesus said, "If ye then, being evil, know how to give good gift unto your children, how much more shall your Father which is in heaven give good things to them that ask him?" (Matt. 7:11).

The Lord invites us to ask the Father for all good things. Faith can get anything in the universe, with nothing impossible.

Faith And Divine Healing

Man is always trying to beat God and will never succeed! There has been so many loose talks about divine healing before the recent revivals of the Holy Ghost Service where miracle of healing are vivid and naked. Though there are still people that are skeptical about the whole move, God is on with his healing business.

Every Christian ought at once to claim perfect healing on the basis of the atonement just as he takes salvation by faith at once. In Deuteronomy 28, sickness is called a curse. Curse come from Satan and blessings (including healing) comes from God. It is an indisputable fact that God's will is our health, but Satan's will is our destruction by disease, misery, sin and early death. God gave all mankind divine health at Calvary. Satan spends his time cheating us by telling us this is a lie, and unfortunately we more often believe Satan's lies than God's truth.

The truth of God is what Isaiah 53:45 declared: "Surely he hath borne our grief and carried sorrows, yet we did esteem him stricken, smitten of God, and afflicted. But he was wounded for our transgressions, he was bruised for our iniquities, the chastisement of our peace was upon him and with his stripes we are healed."

It is foolish to fight the plain teaching of these verses. Jesus Himself took our infirmities and bare our diseases. Each time Satan tries to attack you in any part of your body, immediately claim the appropriate promises, eat it up, make it a substance in your blood stream and in your heart and being the incorruptible seed of God, it will spring up and produce of its kind. If you swallow "by His stripes I am healed," you will find that the seed will produce this in your life and healing brings health.

God is a healing God, the Creator, the Author and giver of life. Everything that exist does so because of God's life. His heart desire for every believer is that you might have good health in abundance. But only on the premises of "asking" and this asking must have faith in it.

The God of heaven heals by the prayer of faith.

Chapter 6

THE MYSTERIES OF PRAYER

THE MYSTERIES OF PRAYER

L et's now see what I called the mysteries of answered and unanswered prayers. First importunity and persistence are a mystery of answered prayer. How?

Mystery Of Answered Prayer

Our Lord taught men to pray to God the Father. That is the central fact of His teaching. He rebuked all parade and pretence in prayer. On a matter which is already freely offered to everybody in the world, it is unbelief and rebellion not to believe God and accept what He offers. He has offered salvation to every person in the roll who will receive it. But on other matters in which we are not sure of His will, it might require our waiting on Him to be certain. Unless we wait on Him, He may not work out His will in our lives. Persistent, believing, intercessory, agonizing prayer is proper for a Christian when he takes his burdens to God.

Importunity and Persistence

There are so many examples of people in the Bible who prayed through by their persistency. We have the record of how Jacob wrestled with God and prevailed. Genesis 32:24-29 narrated this story as follows:

"And Jacob was left alone; and there wrestled a man with him until the breaking of the day. And when he saw that he prevailed not against him, he touched the hollow of his thigh; and the hollow of Jacob's thigh was out of joint, as he wrestled with him. And he said, let me go, except thou bless me.

And he said unto him, what is thy name? And he said, Jacob. And he said, thy name shall be called no more Jacob but Israel; for as a prince hast thou power with God and with men, and has prevailed.

And Jacob asked him, "Tell me, I pray thee, thy name. And he said, wherefore is it that thou doest ask after my name? And he blessed him there."

There is outstanding evidence that Jacob had already trusted in the Lord. He met God at Bethel, described in Genesis 28, but now Jacob prevailed with God and got a new name and new blessing. He went out next morning to meet Esau unafraid after the all-night prayer and wrestling with God.

Jacob certainly prayed through about meeting his blood-thirsty brother, who had sworn to kill him. Christians have a right to pray through about their problems and burdens.

Daniel set his face to seek the Lord by prayer and supplication, with fasting, sackcloth and ashes (Dan. 9:3). He prayed through until the Angel Gabriel came and made known to Daniel the thing he was so greatly concerned

The Mysteries of Prayer

about – the future of the nation of Israel which has sinned against God.

We again have in the tenth chapter, Daniel prayer through three full weeks without eating any pleasant bread, any meat or wine. Finally his prayer was answered and divine revelation was given to him, then his heart's burden was eased.

Nehemiah prayed through about the sad condition of the desolate city of Jerusalem and her walls during the captivity. Nehemiah 1:4 says: "And it came to pass, when I heard these words that I sat down and wept, and mourned certain days, and faster, and prayed before the God of heaven."

Some of Nehemiah's prayer is given to us; how humbly he plead with God! His prayer was heard, the heart of the king was touched, and God sent Nehemiah back to build the wall of the city so dear to his heart because he prayed through.

Some of Nehemiah's prayer is given to us; how humbly he pleaded with God! His prayer was heard, the heart of the king was touched, and God sent Nehemiah back to build the wall of the city so dear to his heart because he prayed through.

When a group of Jews were going back from Babylon to Jerusalem under Ezra the scribe, they proclaimed a fast at the river Ahava. There they afflicted themselves and fasted and prayed and begged God for protection from the bandit bands that roamed the country, since they were ashamed to ask the king for soldiers, having told him that God would care for them. And they prayed through, as Ezra 8:21-23 tell us, and was entreated for them and protect them. They arrived safely and unharmed at Jerusalem.

The Jews fasted and prayed for God to spare their lives during the time of Queen Esther in Persia, and in three days and nights they prayed through and the Jews had salvation and then vengeance on their enemies.

The people of Nineveh fasted and prayed, and God repented of the evil that He has thought to do to their great city and did it not. Their fasting was not in order to get saved but that God would relent and not destroy the great wicked city as He had announced through Jonah.

In the New Testament it is the same way. Preceding Pentecost, it is certainly fair to say that the disciples prayed through. Acts 1:14 says,

"These all continued with one accord in prayer and supplication, with the women, and Mary the mother of Jesus and with His brethren."

Paul the apostle was converted on the road to Damascus. After his conversion he went three days and nights praying and fasting (Acts 9:9,11). Paul prayed through and got his eyesight restored and he was filled with the Holy Ghost to begin his marvelous ministry.

In Acts 13: 1-4 we see again a group of Christians praying through. They ministered unto the Lord and fasted until God told them they should send Barnabas and Saul as missionaries. They prayed through for divine leading. Then again they fasted and prayed for divine power on these preachers and sent them forth.

The twelfth chapter of Acts, verses 1 to 17, we saw how a group of Christians gathered in the home of Mary, the mother of John Mark, and prayed through until apostle Peter was released from Jail by an Angel. That was long-continued, heart- searching, heart-broken praying. And that is the example of New Testament Christians everywhere.

God want His children to wait on Him, hold his hand, and plead for the things they needed, particularly power and help in the things they cannot do themselves. For example, in Lk. 11:5-8, Jesus gave this story:

"And He said unto them which, of you shall have a friend and shall go unto him at midnight, and say unto him, friend, lend me three loaves for a friend of mine in his journey is come to me, and I have nothing to set before him. And he from within shall answer and say, trouble me not; the door is now shut, and my children are with me in bed; I cannot rise and give thee. I say unto you, though he will not rise and give him because he is his friend, yet because of his importunity he will rise and give him as many as he needeth."

Note the key words in verse 8: "Because of his importunity he will rise and give him as many as he needeth. "Importunity is the way to things, from the passage evidently refers to a child of God wanting power either to win others or to do exploit for Him. A believer has a right to go to God and ask for the bread of life to give others.

A born again child of God who want the supernatural miracle working power of the Holy Spirit has a right to wait on God. Yea, is taught to do so by the plain word of our Saviour Himself. Jesus taught importunate prayer in Luke 18:1-8:

"And he spake a parable unto them to this end, that men ought always to pray, and not to faith: Saying, there was in a city a judge, which feared not God, neither regarded man; and there was a widow in that city; and she came unto him, saying, Avenge me of my adversary. And he would not for a while; but afterwards he said within himself, though I fear not God nor regard any man. Yet because this widow troubleth me, I will avenge her lest by her continual coming she weary me. And the Lord said, Hear what the unjust judge saith. And shall not God avenge his own elect, which cry day and night unto Him, though He bears long with them? I tell you that He will avenge them speedily. Nevertheless when the son of man cometh, shall he find faith on the earth?"

The goal of this parable is that of praying through. He spoke a parable "to this end, that men ought always to pray and not faint."

A poor widow came to plead with a judge to hear her cause and deliver her from her adversaries and give her justice. And shall not God's own children who cry unto Him day and night. And shall not God avenge them speedily.

Verse 8 above hints that when the Saviour comes, will He find faith on the earth? People do not believe in prayer. People do not pray through. People do not pay the price in heart-seaching, in long hours, in fasting, in confession, in restitution. But when God's people really pray through, then they can have revival; protection, provision, anointing of the Holy Spirit and anything else God has for His people.

A bonafide child of God has a right to camp on God's doorstep and persistently, insistently plead the promises of God and refuse to take denial, until that which is needed, that which is imperative to win and have revivals, is received from God.

Keep on praying
Till you pray it through
God's great promises
Are always true
Keep on praying
Till you pray it through

The Mystery Of Unanswered Prayer.

Nearly every week someone meets me as a pastor to ask, didn't Jesus says: "Ask, and it shall be given you, seek, and ye shall find, knock, and it shall be opened unto you?" But why is it that I did not receive what I ask for? I sometimes bypass a theological discussion of Jesus' words: Matthew 7:7 and simply ask, what is the prayer you have been praying that you felt God is not answering? Let us get into the root of the matter. It is amazing how often that response open the door for an outing of honest confusion and frustration.

- I have been praying for my husband's conversion but his bad habit is growing worst.
- I have been praying for the fruit of the womb and now my husband family is treating me with divorce.
- I have been trusting God for a life suitor for the past few years and now I am looking older.
- I have been looking for job, but none was fort coming and the economy is growing worst.

The list of these lamentations goes on week after week, month after month, year after year. In fact, I could not count how many people I have counseled about the mystery or the agony of unanswered prayer. And the people who suffer most keenly are those who truly believe that prayer moves mountains.

A very simple outline of God's reaction to prayer are:

- If the request is wrong, God says, "No"
- If the thing is wrong, God says, "Slowdown"
- If the request is right, timing is right and you are right, "Confirmed"

We would look at the first two problems – Wrong request and wrong timings in this chapter and the third problem we would look at in some detail in the next chapter.

Untenable Requests

If the request made is wrong, God says, "No" Some prayer requests, no matter how well intentioned, are inappropriate. Jesus' disciples were not immune from making misguided requests. Not even the three who were closest to Him – Peter, James and John.

These three disciples once accompanied Jesus to the top of a high mountain. Suddenly God's full glory descended upon Jesus, and Moses and Elijah appeared beside Him. Beholding God's splendor just a few feet from where they were standing, Peter, James and John drew back in awe. Then Peter came with a prayer request. Some believe that, loosely translated, his request went like this: "Jesus, let us build shelter up here for you, Moses and Elijah. We would be happy to stay on the mountain with you and be swimming in your glory." Jesus immediate response was effectively, No: a thick cloud enveloped them cutting off further conversation. Jesus and the disciples still had work to do down in the plains where people live. They could not stay on the mountain top. Peter's request was inappropriate, and Jesus would not grant it. The complete story of this prayer request is in (Matt. 17:1; Mark 9:2; Lk. 9:28-36).

Another time James and John came with their mother to Jesus, asking for reservation of the best two seats in His Kingdom. It was not just a show view they were after; they wanted to be Jesus' chief executive officers. "No", was Jesus answer. "You do not know what you are asking for. There is going to be a lot of pain and hardship in my

Kingdom before my glory is revealed. Besides, the places of honour are already reserved." In other words, "your request is inappropriate, and I will not grant it". (The story is recorded in Matt. 20:20-30; Mk. 10:35-40).

James and John seemed to have a knock for requesting the wrong thing. Sometimes after the transfiguration, Jesus and the disciples were denied a travelling permit through a Samaritan town. This setback irritated James and John so much that they asked Jesus to destroy the town with fire from heaven. Once again, Jesus denied their request. In fact, He rebuked them for making such a silly demand (Lk. 9:51-60 tells the story).

His Love Compels Him Not To Say Yes

If the disciples were capable of making wrong request: - request that are totally self-serving, parental materialistic, shortsighted, immature – sometimes so you and I are. Fortunately, our God loves us too much to say yes to inappropriate requests. He will answer such prayers, but His answer is "No." I would not want to serve God who would do less than that. But by hindsight, I thank God for saying "No" to prayers that at times seemed appropriate, but are not.

Motives Is Important

It is not likely, of course, that any of us would want to approach God with the intention of making a wrong request. What are some of these wrong requests we might make without even realizing we are out of line?

The most famous wrong request is this: "O God, please change the other person." Wives make this about husbands, husbands about wives, parents about children, employees about bosses. In fact whenever two or more Christians have to relate closely to each other, somebody is likely to make this request.

Now do not misunderstand my line of focus, it is often perfectly appropriate to pray that someone will change. After all, that is what we do when we pray for conversion, for hearts to be softened, and be broken to permit God residing in the heart. But too often the motive behind such a request is not authentic concern for the other person.

A more genuine prayer might be this: "I do not want to face my own short-comings. I do not want to work on this relationship. I do not want to change at all. I do want to be tender hearted and be sanctifies. Instead, I want the other person to accommodate all my personal needs, so I am asking you to change him/her." If you pray that kind of prayer, God may say "No."

God's Glory or Your Own?

There are plenty of other inappropriate, self- serving prayers masquerading as reasonable requests. "Please give me money and increase my account" may be a good request for business executives. There is nothing wrong in praying for business buoyancy; for we should bring our entire request onto God. But if the motive is to show off or to get rich in order to live lavishly and give the crumbs to God, it is a wrong request and God is likely to say "No."

Pastor may pray, O Lord, help our church to grow. Surely God would want to honour that request! But if the Pastor's real meaning is "I want to be able to be a star with big church, fancy programmes and lots of media coverage," their request are wrong. Likewise, the Christian musicians who pray; "Help my album sell and my concert tour to take shape" may be asking for personal glory, matter how often they refer to God on stage. We can fool ourselves into thinking selfish request are appropriate, but God cannot be fooled. (Gal. 6:7) He knows our motives, and they are destructive, He often protects it from them by saying, No.

Before you bring any request to God it will be proper to ask: If God granted this request,
   *Would it bring glory to Him?
   *Would it advance His Kingdom?
   *Would it help people?
   *Would it help me to grow spiritually?
Working on this question would force us to look closely at our request, prayer can purify us when we conclude that our motives have been wrong, we can say, "Lord forgive me. Help me to grow." Then you also search for his will in His Holy Book in order to present your request in line with His will. If you have been praying diligently about a matter and have sensed resistance from heaven, I challenge you to review your request. It may be the problem. May be your request is not straight forward, an unwillingness to face the real issue. May be it is destructive

in a way you do not understand. May be it is self-serving. Shortsighted or too small. God may have something better in mind. Whatever the reason if the request is wrong, God says "No!"

Another consideration about prayer is that, if timing is wrong God says, "Slow down." For most of us, this is not better than "No". We live in the civilized world of instant everything, always want to do everything faster. Expressway are created around, express film processors, express dry cleaners, express marriages, and many other express this and that. That explains why people have complained to Pastors, "I do not know what to do, I have been praying and fasting for something for three days now, and God has not done it."

God cannot be intimated by childish demand for instant gratification than wise parents are. He simply shakes his head at our immaturity and says; "kick the blocks and scram if you must, but you cannot have what you want yet. I know what I am doing, I have my reasons."

Our Father Knows All Things

Many children hate to hear the answer, "Not yet." And there is an impatient child in all of us, a child who want God to meet every need, grant every request, and move every mountain right now, if not yesterday. When the all-knowing, all-wise, loving heavenly Father deems it is best to say "Not yet." Our self-made nature adult response is like this: "But God, you do not understand, I want it now, You are weary of insisting that you know much better than God about when a prayer request should be granted. God's delays are necessarily denials. He has reason for His not yet.

God is a loving who will give us what and when we need it. Do not think of Him as a Celestial Vending machine that we could kick if we do not get instant response. We must be able to trust His loveliness even if we do not see immediate result.

Sometimes God delays so that we modify our requests. Over time we may see the original request was not quite legitimate. As we understand the situation better, we may want to modify it to make it in line with God's will.

At other times God delays so that we can develop character qualities such as endurance, trust, patience or submission, qualities that come only when we wait patiently and trust in His timing. A lot of spiritual gains come our way, though, how long would any of us put up with these character builders without asking God to remove them.

We may not be able to see the reasons for the delay, but that should not be surprising. As God says in Isaiah 55:8-9 that: "For my thoughts are not your thoughts, neither are your ways my ways saith the Lord. For as the heavens are higher than the earth, so are my ways higher than your ways, and my thoughts than your thoughts." We are the creatures; God is the creator. He knows what timing is best as they say "God's time is the best."

There is one other reason our prayers may not be answered. It is possible that something is wrong in our life that we have set up some barrier between ourselves and God. God repeatedly invites us to come to him with all our needs. He offers us free access to all His resources. But our hangovers have to be cleared up before taking Him up on His offer.

Prayer Saboteurs

Suppose you are asked by someone about what motivates you to develop your personal prayer life, how would you answer? What are those things that drive you to your knees and make you want to pray more? What makes your prayers more fervent? For me, the greatest prayer motivator is answered prayer. When I pray about conversion of souls and miracle on a MESSAGE I AM ABOUT TO GIVE AND I SEE God confirming it. I am motivated to pray about the next engagement. When I pray about a difficult decision and then I made the best choice. I am motivated to pray about all decisions that come my way.

And when I pray about a need that cannot be met by any human means and God melt it through His miracle-working power, I am motivated to get down on my knees and pray for all kinds of needs, whether personal, ministry/church related or global.

When Heaven Gives No Response

Answered prayers really motivates me, and I think it make everyone feel like Moses on the mountain with his arm upraised directing the battle through his prayers. When my prayers have those kinds of demonstrable result, it is exiting to pray.

But contrast, my prayer life takes a down turn when I am praying diligently, fervently and trustingly without any tangible result or testimonies to show forth for answered prayers. You phone heaven and no-one seems to be at home. The troops are getting massacred before your eyes, and you feel like towering your arms to say of what use is the stretched arms.

In the last chapter, we looked at two major reasons why prayers are unanswered, the request may be inappropriate and the timing may be inadequate. We then promised to look in greater depth at a third reason for unanswered prayer; that is, there may be problem in the life of the person who is praying. When it is unlikely that all your requests are inappropriate, even though some may very well be, or it is unlikely that your timing is always off balance, even though sometimes you may push ahead of God. It is more likely that some malfunction in your life is blocking your prayers, even the appropriate, well-timed ones.

When prayers are not answered, most people want to know what is wrong with God. This is normal human response. It is a lot easier to blame God than to look in the mirror of His word and say, "May be I am the problem. Only few people have the courage and sincerity to say I might be the obstacles to the miracle I am praying for." Based on His promises in the few listed Biblical reasons for unanswered prayer, it has something to do with the life of the person praying.

Everything By Prayer

The most common cause of unanswered prayer is PRAYERLESSNESS. As James 4:2 says: "Ye have not, because ye ask not." Be honest with yourself. How often does something like this happen? You decide to pray about something. You add it to your prayer points, list or tell a prayer partner that you are praying about it and you almost do. But though you think about it from time to time, you hardly do any serious praying about it. Why is God not answering your prayer? It might be because you have not yet prayed purposefully, fervently, expectantly. People often say that they have claimed Biblical promises, and prayed fasted or even agreed with other believer friend but the answers to their prayer were not forth coming. Have you really pray regularly and fervently over an extended period of time.

When was the last time you prayed diligently over a period of time:

- For your wife, your husband, your parents, your children?
- For someone to know Christ or to be born again?
- For your Spiritual leader?
- For your Nation and your leader?
- For peace in the war-torn parts of our world?

That Africa will bring a revolution to Christendom and usher in the Lord?

That God will use you for promoting His revival and glory?

I have heard it said that if you bring a cup to God. He will fill it. If you bring a bucket to God, He will fill that. If you bring a big tank to God, He will fill that too. Are you expecting God to fill your needs? Are you asking Him to do so regularly, earnestly and persistently? His name is El-Shaddai.

Polluted By Cheating

The second reason for unanswered prayer is the most obvious. UNCONFESSED SIN – cuts off our communication with the Father. As Isaiah 59:2 says; "But your iniquities have separated between you and your God, and your sins have hid his face from you, which he will not hear."

What kind of sins cut off our access to God?

The prophet Malachi spoke against cheating God, or stealing His share; non-payment of tithes and commensurate offerings to Him. Despite God's clear instructions to offer only the best animals as sacrifices to the Lord, Israelites were taking their prize animals to market where they could get the top prize for them. Then they took the worthless animals – the blind, the lame that are ready to die – and brought them to God's altar.

Besides attempting to cheat God, Israel leaders were cheating the poor. They were absurdly low wages, making life economically difficult for the widows and strangers. (Mal. 3:5). In addition they were also treating their wives with divorce. "You weep and wail because (the LORD) no longer pays attention to your offerings or accept them with pleasure from your hands. You ask "why" it is because they are acting as witness between you and the wife of your youth, because you have broken faith with her, though you live together and she is your partner, the wife of your marriage covenant." (Mal.2:13-14)

Through Malachi, God exclaimed! After cheating me, the oppressed among you, and even your wives, you have the audacity to ask for my favour! You mock me, and then you expect me to grant your requests! But why should I honour your request when you don't honour mine? (Malachi 1).

Any speck of dirt could cause a loss of power. If you let a little sin into your heart, it is going to contaminate your prayers. Your Christian life will not achieve its full potentials. God expect us to maintain a strict personal integrity and undiluted Holiness. We are to show thoughtfulness and love towards others and to maintain a relationship with Him. "What does the Lord require of you? To act justly, love mercy and to walk humbly with your God." (Matt. 6:8). If we refuse to do these things, we are presumptuous to expect God to answer our prayer. If you are tolerating sin in your life, do not waste your breath praying unless it is a prayer of confession.

Unhealthy Relationship

The third prayer insulator is UNRESOLVED RELATIONAL CONFLICT, Matthew 5:23-24 says: "Therefore if thou bring thy gift to the altar and there remembers that thy brother hath ought against thee, leave there thy gift before the altar, and go thy way; first be reconciled to thy brother, and then come and offer thy gift."

I Peter 3:7 extend this principle:

"Ye husbands, dwell with them (your wives) according to knowledge, giving honour unto thy wife, as unto the weaker vessel, and as being heirs together of the grace of life, that your prayer be not hindered."

Most of us grossly underestimate how committed God is to building and maintaining a loving community. He adopts us into His family, and He wants us to carry out relationship with Him into our relationship with others. If we do good to our brothers and sisters, it is like doing good to Jesus Himself (Matt 25:31-46). Since God has forgiven us we should forgive others (Ephesians 4:32; Col. 3:13). There is no point in praying if we are engaged in on-going conflict with a family member, a co-worker, a neighbor, a friend, "He that saith he is in the light and hateth his brother, is in darkness even until now." (I John 2:9). God will listen to you when you come into the light, confess the sin that drove you and the other person apart and mend the relationship. This is what is called restitution.

Of course restitution is always difficult to carry out but it must be done. Romans 12:18 says "If it be possible, as such as lieth in you, live peaceably with all men." Sometimes, the other person would sincerely restore this relationship, or are you holding something back? If attempt have been wholehearted and honest, God will definitely intervened.

Narrow Focus

SELFISHNESS: Is the fourth saboteur. "When you ask and you do not receive because you ask with wrong motives, that you may spend what you get on your pleasures." (James 4:3) Many of the inappropriate requests are wrong because they are selfish. Selfishness in the heart is a very common barrier between prayer and God. How would you feel if your prayer request were made public, displayed on a notice board? Dear Lord, I ask that you make me famous, make me rich quickly, and make sure I have good time. Keep me from stress and anything that will make me grow and become a man of God. Just give me a convenient, happy, satisfying, problem free life. Then, there will be no need to pray.

When Jesus prayed the model prayer we now call the Lord's prayer, His first request were that God's name be revered, that His kingdom come, that His will be done, that does not sound much like self-centered, shortsighted prayers many of us are involved in. If God granted some of our patently selfish requests, we should quickly be spiritually destroyed.

Failure To Listen To The Poor

The fifth prayer saboteur is UNCARING ATTITUDES. Proverbs 21:23 says, "Whosoever stops his ear at the cry of the poor; he also shall cry himself but shall not be heard." A beautiful passage in the Old Testament is about this prayer insulator. Israel was wondering why God was not answering their prayers. They even fasted and humbled themselves, but God did not listen to them. Please, see Isaiah 58:3-9.

God is committed to developing a people who will reflect His character in this world, and His character always expressed concern and compassion for afflicted.

As just one person you may not be able to change the world, but you can however, look for a small difference in today's evils of unemployment, illiteracy, alcoholism and harlotry. If your ear is opened to the afflicted, God will keep His ear open to you.

Unconcerned Toward His Word

If your prayer does not get to God, then the happy fellowship, oneness of purpose, communication between you and God is hindered. This could be caused by the sixth saboteur - UNCONCERNED or nonchalance toward the word of God. Proverbs 23:9 says; "He that turned away his ear from hearing the law, even his prayer shall be abomination."

If your heart is turned away from the Bible, if you have unconcerned attitude to read it, if it is not interesting to you, if you do not meditate on it prayerfully, joyfully, then your prayer has no substance.

God stresses the fact, in His holy book that there is a close connection between the word of God and spiritual prosperity. Psalm 1:1-3 tells us of the blessed man who dislike evil companions. "His delight is in the law of the Lord; and in His law doth he meditate day and night. And he shall be like a tree planted by the rivers of water, that bringeth forth fruit in his season; his leaf also shall not wither; and whatsoever he doeth shall prosper."

Day to day blessing from God, Good success, Christian fruit bearing all depend upon delighting in the law of the Lord and meditating on it day and night. Knowing the Bible is not enough, reading it is not enough; blessing depends on delighting in it and meditation on it (Joshua 1:8). How could one who is non-charlatan to the Bible, who shuns it, one who has his heart turn from it, please God in prayer? What claims could such an unspiritual heart, such an alienated child, have on God in prayer? Such a Christian cannot meet any of the conditions of successful prayer. Oh! Dear believer, if your heart has been turned away to meet any of the conditions of successful prayer. Oh! Dear believer, if your hearts has been turned away from the Bible, you are out of touch with the promises of God of answers to prayers! The blessed Holy Spirit has an affirmation for the word of God. The natural mind is a stranger to God and is not interested and the keenest delight in the word of God. The natural mind is a stranger to god and is not interested in His book. And the carnal or the untaught and the unspiritual Christian is likely to have no taste for God's word. The non-charlatan to God's word is an unspiritual state, a state of backsliding and sin.

Therefore, to get your prayers on the course, will mean to search out His will and quote authority from Christ giving you the right to ask in His name. Delight in His word. God is so revealed in the word and your line to glory will be expressway.

The Wrong Key

INADEQUATE FAITH is the final prayer saboteur. "If any of you lack wisdom, let him ask of God, that giveth to all men liberally and upbraideth not; let him ask in faith, nothing wavering. For he that wavereth is like a wave of the sea driven with the wind and tossed. For let not that man think that he shall receive anything of the Lord. A double- minded man is unstable in all his ways." (James 1:5-8).

God is able. He is omnipotent. If you do not know that doctrine, you might as well forget about prayer. If your prayer has cloud of doubt hanging over them, you can as well strike them out, because they will not get anywhere.

Before going down to your knees go to scripture, and look at what God has done for His people. Then review His performance record in your life; looking for the evidence of His power, His faithfulness, and His provision. Tune your mind properly so that when you finally pray, it will be to a Glorious God who is able.

The more you are convinced of God's ability, the more He demonstrates His ability to you. Jesus never tells his followers to throw wishes heavenwards. Instead He says, "For verily I say unto you, that whosoever shall say unto this mountain, be thou removed and be thou cast into the sea, and shall not doubt in his heart, but shall believe that those things which he saith shall come to pass; he shall have whatsoever he saith."(Mark 11:23). When you pray, also put a plan in place on seeing demonstration of God's mighty power.

Yes To Our Prayers.

If the truth were known, often you and I are the only obstacles standing in the way of us receiving desperately needed miracles. Our request may be right. The timing may not be a problem. But when our lives are wrong, God says, before I grant your request, I want you to grow more. Put that sin away. Change your attitude. Stop that practice, end that pattern, get away from merry-go-round, reconcile that relationship, soften up your spirit, repent, receive forgiveness. Grow more and I will "throw open the gates of heaven and pour out so much blessing that you will not have room enough for it." (Mal. 3:10)

Probably none of us can understand how much God wants to change that impossible circumstance, touch that untouchable person, move the unmovable mountain in our needs and grant our requests if we will free Him to do it. When our request is right, when the timing is right and when the person is right, God says. Yes!

Nothing motivates people to develop their prayer lives more than answered prayers. And once the prayer saboteurs are dealt with and dispatched, the way is clear for God to answer one prayer after another. We have a Mighty God who specializes in impossibilities; nothing is too hard for Him. He cares and loves us. He wants us to have all our needs and desire.

Chapter **7**

GOD'S LINE
IS
NEVER ENGAGED

GOD'S LINE IS NEVER ENGAGED

God's telephone line is His hotline. His direct line never get busy; you can access Him all the time whether in the day or in the night. His business is to take care of you and yours. If you could ask God for one miracle in your life, knowing that he would grant your request, wouldn't you ask Him?

*To bring a loved one to Christ
*To heal your body
*To put your scattered marriage back together
*To break your financial hardship
*To change something about your job
*To bring home your straying son or daughter
*To be more zealous and Holy in your walk with God.

What your request might be, do it regularly and with all diligence, every single day, bring it on line with God on Telephone, trusting that He will intervene in your situation. If you have not been doing so, why not start today.

He Is Capable To Handle It

Most of us have to admit that we are too casual and we do not often pray about our deepest needs. We are faint-hearted. We begin to pray, but found ourselves drifting mentally during prayer times, using empty phrases. Our words sounds hallow and shallow and we start to feel hypocritical.

Soon we give up. It seems better to live with almost any difficult situation than to continue to pray ineffectively.

We reach to God, because we know He is holding out arms towards us. But then we often fall back and try to face our difficulties in our own power, because at some basic and perhaps unconscious level we doubt if God really make a difference in the problem we are facing. It is well and good to believe that God loves us and want to help us. Indeed He is capable to do so.

Only Believe

Many of us have passing personal needs and serious problems that ravage our lives, but we do not ask God for help because somewhere, well beneath our surface layer of faith and trust, we do not believe God has power to do anything about them.

The fact is the God is able to handle any problems we bring unto Him. Creating planet is not much of a problem for Him. Neither is raising the dead. Nothing, absolutely nothing is too difficult for God to handle, but He is waiting for us to recognize His power and ask for help.

So launch an assault on your lack of conviction; open the Bible and locate every passage in Old and New Testament that emphasized God's ability to accomplish anything He desires.

Look for passage that demonstrates God's power over nature. When God decided certain seas or rivers need parting, He parted them (Ex. 4:35-41). When His troops needed more time to consolidate their gains, He extended the daylight hours (Hos. 10:12-14).

Another interesting story was about Moses' frustration when his people were thirsty (Exod. 17:1-7). He brought their need for water to God, and God said "see that rock?" One can imagine Moses saying "yes" but then what does rock has to do with water? If we need water let us look at the ground.

Read and reread all those stories about God's power over nature until you are convinced that they really happen in History.

His Ability over Circumstances

Next you look at God's ability to change impossible circumstances. When the Holy Ghost came to the believers at the first Pentecost, many went out and preached that Christ had come back from the dead and that He was the Saviour of the world. As a result, thousands of people were converted to the new Christian movement. This made both the Romans officials and the traditional Jewish leaders nervous. Threatened by the crowds' traditional enthusiastic response to the Christian preachers, they feared losing their authority over them.

And so the Roman and Jewish leaders resisted the movement. They arrested several prominent Christians and killed them publicly. This did no good at all; the Christians said they could not help speaking what they have seen and heard.

Next, the officials captured, tortured and imprisoned some of the disciples. This had no lasting effect either, once released, the disciples spoke with even greater boldness about Finally, Herod Agrippa, Jerusalem's governor arrested the apostle James, the brother of John, an elder in the apostolic church, and executed him. He then laid plans to put Peter to death also (Acts 12).

Unfortunately for Herod's plan, he had Peter arrested during the Passover feast. To protect Jewish traditions, he could not execute the apostle during Passover week, so Peter was left to spend several days in the prison before losing his head.

To be sure other Christian would not spring their leader; Herod made Peter's security tight. Sixteen Roman Soldiers were assigned to guard him. He was chained to the left and to the right. Sentries guarded the entrance to the cell.

Peter's fellow-Christians did not get together to plan a prison break-out. They know all human tactics would be futile. Instead they prayed. But Peter remained in prison, and his trial date approached.

Surprised At Answer

The night before the trial and execution, the Christians met at the home of Mary, the mother of John Mark, to hold an all-night prayer vigil. Peter vigil. Peter was confident in Christ whether he lived or dies, he slept deeply between his captors.

"And behold, an Angel of the Lord came upon him, and a light shined in the prison, and he smote Peter on His side, and raised him up saying, "arise up quickly". And the chains fell off from his hands. And the Angel said unto him, guard thyself and bind on thy sandals. And so he did. And he said unto him, cast thy garment about thee, and follow me. And he went out and followed him; and whist not that it was true which was done by the Angel; but thought he saw a vision. When they were past the first and the second ward, they came unto Iron Gate that leadeth unto the city, which opened to them of his own accord, and they went out, and passed on through one street and forthwith the Angel departed from him." (Acts 12:7-10).

Baffled, Peter looked around him, "was this real"? "was he free"? Had an Angel really opened those prison doors? The truth dawned on him and he made way to where the believers are gathered praying. A servant answered his knock. Hearing his voice, she squealed with joy and ran back to tell the praying saints that their prayers were answered.

"And they said unto her, thou art mad. But she constantly affirmed that it was even so. Then said they, it is an Angel. But Peter continued knocking and when they had open the door, and saw him, they were astonished." (Acts 12:15-16).

First century Christians were nothing different from the twentieth-century Christians to think that God may not miraculously re-arrange circumstances in answer to prayer, but they prayed anyway. And God rewarded their somewhat incomplete faith, not by sending them comforting visions, but by altering history.

He Has Control Over Lives

Also you need to look at the passages that reveal God's power to change people's hearts.

God had the power to make shy Moses a leader (Exod. 3:4), to soften cruel people's hearts (Exod. 11:1-8), to keep discouraged Elijah from quitting (I Kings 19:10-18), to turn the fanatical persecutor Saul into a globe-totting apostle (Acts 9:1-31).

Looking again at the apostle Peter, we see the tremendous difference God's power made in his life. While imprisoned, Peter was so full of faith and peace that he could sleep deeply, even though they thought he would be killed the next day. Ten or fifteen years earlier, Peter had been a different man.

When Jesus was captured in the middle of the night and dragged before religious and civil authorities, most of the disciples ran away in terror, Peter, to his credit followed his Master right into the high priest's courtyard. But there he lost heart. "They are going to kill him," he thought, "and then they will start looking for His friends. I should better pretend and disguise that I did not know Him."

Jesus knew Peter would deny Him, and He also knew that Peter the coward, through God's mighty power, would become Peter the rock, the first major leader of the Christian church (Matt. 16:18-19).

"Simon, Simon", Jesus said to Peter the very night of the arrest and denial, "Satan had determined to sift you as wheat. But I have prayed for you, Simon, that your faith may not fail. And when you have turned back strengthen your brothers." (Luke 22:31-32).

After the crucifixion, Peter was a broken man. He could not put the pieces back together by himself. Only God's Pentecostal power could change him, and the power did it, as we see throughout the book of Acts.

We should study God's power in human lives until our being saturated with the conviction that God had His was whenever he desired – in anyone's life he wanted to change and that those things happened in history not mythology.

The Same Yesterday, Today And Forever

We must study those passages in order to own the doctrines of God's Omnipotence in history. Not minding what the people think or the scholars' opinions. We must be firm in our faith that God immutability is firmly established by Biblical passage such as: Malachi 3:6. "Jesus Christ the same yesterday, today and forever." God has not changed. He is not growing old, and His power is not waning. "Has thou not known? Hast thou not heard that the everlasting God, the Lord, the Creator of the ends of the earth, fainteth not, neither is weary? There is no searching of his understanding." (Isaiah 40:28). If He ever was able to control nature, change people and alter circumstances, He is still able to do these things.

The Bible is repeating these words over and over that "God is able." He is able to save three of His followers from fiery furnace (Dan. 3:17); able to save Daniel from Lion's mouths

(Dan. 6:20-21); able to give a child to ninety-year old Sarah (Rom. 4:18- 21); able to give His followers all that they need. (II Cor. 9:8). The Lord is able to save completely those who come to Him through Jesus (Heb. 7:25) and able to do immeasurably more than all we ask or imagine (Eph. 3:20).

Whatever it takes for you to own the doctrine of God's Omnipotence, do it. Until you own it, you will be faint-hearted in prayer. You will make a few wishes on your knees, but you would not be able to persevere in prayer until you know in your heart that God's telephone line is never engaged.

A prayer warrior is a person who is convinced that God is Omnipotent that He has the power to do anything, to change anything and to intervene in any circumstance. A person who truly believes this refuses to doubt God.

You Are Personally Invited

God is eager to pour this good gift out upon us. Now we know that not only is He willing; He is also able to bless beyond what we can imagine. But some of us are still hanging back, reluctant to crash uninvited into the presence of the King of the universe.

Hang back no longer! God, through Christ, has issued you a personal invitation to Telephone Him anytime, because it is heavenly digitalized and its direct to His room. In fact, it is impossible to call His room uninvited, but because His word tells us to "pray continually." (I Thess. 5:17).

If you are not a born-again Christian yet, God's invitation says this:

"Come unto me, all ye that labour and are heavy laden and I will give you rest. Take my yoke upon you, and learn of me; for I am meek and lowly in heart: and ye shall find rest unto your souls."

If you are already God's child, the invitation is wide open. You can pray about anything; "Be careful for nothing; but in everything by prayer and supplication with thanksgiving let you request be made known unto God." (Phil. 4:6).

You can pray wherever you are; "I will therefore that men pray everywhere, lifting up holy hands, without wrath and doubting." (I Tim. 2:8).

You do not need to be afraid or timid: "Let us therefore come boldly unto the throne of grace; that we may obtain mercy, and find grace to help in time of need." (Heb. 4:16).

Although you pray in Jesus' Name you can be sure that your requests go directly to God: "And that day ye shall ask in my name and I say not unto you, that I will pray unto the Father for you; for the Father himself loveth you because ye have loved me, and have believed that I come out from God." (John 16:26-27).

It would be foolish not to accept God's invitation: "Ye have not because ye ask not." (John 4:2).

When you accept God's invitation, miracles, signs and wonders begin to happen. You would not believe the changes that will occur in your life – in your marriage, your family, your business, career, your ministry and church, your witnessing and so on – once you are convinced in the heart of your heart that God is willing, that He is able and that He invited you to come before His throne and do business in prayer.

He's Waiting for Your Phone Call

God is interested in your prayer phone call because He is interested in you. Whatever matters to you is a priority for His attention. Nothing in the universe matters as much as to Him as what is going on in your life this day. You do not have to pester Him to get His attention. You do not have to use any trick or gymnastics to show you really mean business. He is your father. He wants to hear what you have to say. In fact, He is waiting for your phone call.

What in God's life is more important to Him, than meeting your need? You are a sensitive issue in the programme of God; it gives God greater pleasure supplying your needs. Each time He asks you on His Telephone receiver. What can I do for you?

"Come into my presence," says God. "Talk to me on my direct line. Share your concerns. I am keenly interested in you because I am your Father. I am able to help, because all power in Heaven and Earth is mine. And I am waiting very eagerly, hoping you will telephone my room in Glory."

BIBLIOGRAPHY

Samuel Chadwick: Path of Prayer, Hodde & Stoughton Ltd. London John R. Rice: Prayer is Asking and Receiving, Sword of the Lord Publishers, Murfressboro, Tennesse Bill Hybels: Slowing Down To Be With God, Inter-vasity Press. Downers Grove, Illinois.

OTHER BOOKS BY THE AUTHOR

1. Christian Education in 21ˢᵗ Century
2. Billionaires Capsules
3. Power of Positive Prayer
4. The Chronicles behind Poverty in the Third World
5. Common Sense of your eating Habits
6. The race of Excellence
7. Divine Capsules for Life
8. Legacy for the succeeding Generation
9. Turning your Loses to Learning
10. Dream
11. Critical thinking
12. Vacancy in the hall of faith
13. The Last Command GO!
14. On a Mission to this Generation
15. Module of mandate for missions.
16. Advancing in God's call.
17. The venture of integrity.
18. The Past, The Present, The Future
19. The Race. The Rehearsal and the Ring
20. The everlasting love of God
21. Repositioning for Kingdom relevance
22. Habits of outstanding people.
23. Unlocking your destiny

Printed in the United States
By Bookmasters